AWOL

OTHER BOOKS BY FRANK SCHAEFFER

Nonfiction

Keeping Faith—A Father-Son Story About Love and the United States Marine Corps (Coauthored with Sgt. John Schaeffer, USMC)

Faith of Our Sons—A Father's Wartime Diary

Voices from the Front—Letters Home From America's Military Family

Fiction

Baby Jack—a novel

The Calvin Becker Trilogy of novels:

Portofino
Zermatt
Saving Grandma

www.FrankSchaeffer.com
www.roth-douquet.com

AWOL

THE UNEHCUSED ABSENCE OF AMERICA'S UPPER CLASSES
FROM THE MILITARY—AND HOW IT HURTS OUR COUNTRY

Kathy Roth-Douquet and Frank Schaeffer

Collins
An Imprint of HarperCollinsPublishers

Note: The opinions expressed by the service members quoted in this book are their opinions only. They should not be construed to represent the official position of any particular branch of service or the Department of Defense.

HarperCollins books may be purchased for educational, business, or sales promotional use. For information please write: Special Markets Department, HarperCollins Publishers, 10 East 53rd Street, New York, NY 10022.

FIRST EDITION

Book design by Daniel Lagin

Library of Congress Cataloging-in-Publication Data

Roth-Douquet, Kathy, 1964–
    AWOL : the unexcused absence of America's upper classes from the military—and how it hurts our country / by Kathy Roth-Douquet and Frank Schaeffer.
        p. cm.
    ISBN-13: 978-0-06-088859-6
    ISBN-10: 0-06-088859-8
    1. Military service, Voluntary—United States.   2. United States—Armed Forces—Recruiting, enlistment, etc.   3. Upper class—United States—History—21st Century.   4. Elite (Social sciences)—United States—History—21st century.   5. United States—Social conditions—21st century.   I. Schaeffer, Frank.   II. Title.

UB323.R68 2006
355.2'23620973—dc22   2005056354

06   07   08   09   10   WBC/RRD   10   9   8   7   6   5   4   3   2   1

KATHY'S DEDICATION

To Greg, my hero

and

To Sophie and Charley

FRANK'S DEDICATION

To Genie, Jessica, Dani,

Francis, John, and Becky,

who have all found a way to serve others

Contents

★★☆★

Foreword

★ ★ ★ ★

AWOL is powerful and compelling. It is sure to spark dialogue on issues of patriotism and service to our country. The book is both a love story and a hard-hitting account of military life.

Frank Schaeffer and Kathy Roth-Douquet write from a very personal perspective—Frank's son has served numerous combat tours as a Marine, and Kathy's husband is currently serving—again—in combat as a Marine pilot. When they tell their stories, the authors grapple with personal feelings of love and anxiety as they wrestle several of the most important social issues of our time:

> *Are the higher socioeconomic groups of American society adequately represented in the military? Does it matter?*
> *Do mainstream media evidence cultural arrogance and bias in their reporting about our military? If so . . . so what?*
> *Does it matter that America has a dwindling number of elected leaders with military service?*

AWOL is written with warmth and genuine respect for those who serve. The authors pose the questions—the answers may surprise you.

I am impressed not only by the personal style of this work, but also by the research. This book is fact—not fiction. When we look for balance in a dangerous and complex world, *AWOL* is a good place to start.

—General Tommy Franks (Retired)

AWOL

Introduction

★ ★ ★ ★ ★

Frank and Kathy

We never served in the military. And we certainly claim no personal credit for the fact our respective son and husband volunteered—if it had been up to us initially, they probably wouldn't have. We were raised in a culture, a privileged culture, that misunderstands and underestimates the meaning of military service.

As we came to understand and appreciate the military, it was striking to us how enormous our previous ignorance had been, and how entirely comfortable we had been with that ignorance. And we noticed that we were not alone. People like us—educated, urban, in careers where you make good money, and interested in the good life, good food, travel—entire extended communities of people like us, know nothing about the military.

We are trying to make the case here that this ignorance is not okay, that serving in the military should not be just about personal preference. This is particularly important now when even the leaders of the major institutions in the United States seem not to believe this, when they ask so much of the military, and yet have not asked anyone to serve. It is as if our leaders have become shy of talking about the common duties of citizenship, shy of even using a word like *duty*.

Frank

I guess that this book is Kathy's and my attempt to figure out what happened to us. It is also a declaration of love for a husband and a son and a statement of respect for the choice they made. The Marines borrowed my boy and returned him a man, and in the process made me a little bit better person. My son grew up during five years of service and two combat tours. So did I.

I was extremely fortunate to meet Kathy. Here was a "sister" who was also relatively new to the military family. Here was a splendidly educated and articulate career woman, dedicated mother and military wife, who shared my belief that the growing gap between many civilians and the military is a bad thing. The idea of teaming up to write something together seemed very natural when I learned that Kathy was writing pieces for *USA Today* on the same subject I had been addressing in some of my books and *Washington Post* articles: life within the contemporary military family.

Maybe this book is also—for me, at least—a penance, an "I'm sorry" to the good people who have been protecting me all along. I guess my attitude had been something like that of the hobbits in Tolkien's Middle Earth, as described in *The Lord of the Rings* trilogy. When the hobbits occasionally met the so-called rangers, they were suspicious of them more often than not. The hobbits had no idea what lay beyond their cozy world or any inkling of the price the rangers were paying as they kept vigil. The protectors held a dark universe of terror at bay while the blissfully ignorant and protected slept.

Kathy

I met Frank Schaeffer when he came to a book signing in my town. Like many people in the military, I'm a fan of Frank's work, especially *Keeping Faith* (written with his Marine son John) and *Faith of Our Sons: A Father's Wartime Diary*. He was the only person I knew describing what I experienced, the "disconnect" between my old life and the military world. Frank and I ended up talking for several hours, in between him signing books and me chasing my children around in the bookstore. We compared notes about our "drafting" into the military, about our own previous misconceptions, and those of our friends. We also talked about how much we've benefited, felt honored even, by our experiences. Later in e-mail exchanges we started to talk about the need for a book to help address and maybe even bridge the gap between the military family and the rest of our country.

During my kids' spring break in 2005, I was in Washington, D.C., to do research for this book. People asked me how I was, and I struggled to convey the answer. The kids were missing their dad since he deployed to the war in Iraq. My son hadn't been sleeping through the night, which meant I had gotten up as often as five times a night for nearly two months, and at age forty that gets a bit old. It's hard to keep the routine going, hard to put a sit-down dinner in front of a three- and seven-year-old, hard to read a story and sing a song at the end of a long day by yourself. The older one sometimes tests for discipline. Sometimes I get angrier than I'd like or turn on a movie for the kids a little too often. Sometimes it's hard to fall asleep at night.

I could say all those things, and people would nod sympathetically.

What was harder to say was that I found it was a privilege to hold my family together so my husband could go to war, because our country and our president—even one I didn't vote for—asked him to do so. Through the mechanisms of democracy, the country had asked something of us, and we answered, and it felt like an honor.

It's hard to say the latter part of this "speech" because I know how foreign it sounds to people with professional, upper-middle-class lives. I know how much of these lives are oriented around preventing the kind of uncertainty and risk that my children and I experience, let alone what my husband experiences. This book is Frank's and my attempt to bring people to a place where statements like the one above make sense.

Frank and Kathy

In 2001 we were attacked. In 2005, for the first time in a decade, the U.S. Army fell far short of its recruiting goals, though by the end of that fiscal year the numbers were better than in the spring.[1] Yet President Bush did not use his bully pulpit to urge anyone, much less students at our elite schools, to volunteer. Surely he, as commander in chief, might properly have made such a call.

After 9/11 the *New York Times* endorsed the invasion of Afghanistan as a "just war." They said that our troops were going into battle carrying the hopes and prayers of the *Times*'s editors with them. But they did not ask anyone to share in the responsibility for fighting this new war against Islamic jihadists. Perhaps they did not want the awesome responsibility of suggesting a person actually go to war. Perhaps, though they believed the war was theoretically just, the idea of someone actually fighting it simply made them too uncomfortable.

The president did not make a call. And to our knowledge no major newspaper did. No one in a leadership position made such a

---

1. While the Marine Corps missed some targets for the initial sign-up of recruits, they continued to overperform on the measure that is more critical to them: the number of recruits who actually ship to boot camp. The Army was seriously underperforming both on original sign-ups and shipping-out rates, even after adjusting down their recruiting goals.

call. Maybe the president, the editors of the *Times,* and other national leaders refrained from a call to arms because they didn't want
their own military-aged children to serve.

These days some members of our upper classes are so hostile to
the idea of service that they have all but banned military recruiters
from our best private high schools and college campuses, lest anyone
even suggest to their young people that military service is an honorable interruption in the rush to elite colleges and socially acceptable
jobs and lots of money. The privileged learn that war is bad and believe that those who find themselves in the military—while we "support them"—are likely to be underprivileged, certainly somewhat
suspect, possibly over-avid gun collectors or victims of unscrupulous
recruiters. So why would someone with other good options possibly
choose service?

We have learned that service can be about what America aspires
to be. It can be the melting pot, a meritocracy, and a level playing
field. It can be about what it means to be free and American and
responsible for your neighbor. For young people it can be about
building self-confidence and being given amazing responsibilities at
an age when many young people think it is a big deal to operate a
fax machine at an unpaid internship or that life is "unfair" because
they don't like their college roommate. Last but not least, military
service is also a realistic, often necessary and democratic response to
aggression and chaos.

Undoubtedly there will be readers who disagree—what about
the torturing of prisoners, the raping of Air Force Academy
women, the post-traumatic stress suffered by returning veterans?
It's true—the military is not exempt from crime or tragedy or bad
behavior, even institutional bad behavior. The military, like every
other institution, is located on planet earth and filled with frail
human beings.

There are about one and a half million men and women in

the armed forces, more if you count everyone in the reserves, let alone their dependents. Out of a city of several million souls one would expect some very bad apples. We need to police our institutions, military or civil, scrutinize power structures, and prosecute bad actors. We need the media to tell the truth, even when it embarrasses us. But we need to remember that the failures of military people, and their occasional crimes, aren't an indictment of the military as a whole any more than a congressional bribery scandal should lead people to no longer want to vote—or run for office.

Others will counter that service can be tedious, unpleasant, even fatal. We are not suggesting that everyone will have a wonderful, Outward Bound–type "growth experience" in the military. As a famous Marine Corps recruiting poster of the 1970s said, "We never promised you a rose garden." Any number of people, no doubt, can complain at length about the bad time they had in the armed services. Novels like *Catch-22* draw their inspiration from reality, after all. But the point is exactly as the poster put it—this isn't about choosing a vacation destination. It's about service. And having lived both sides of the civil-military divide, we are struck by how little understood service is, especially by the upper classes.

It was not always this way. Our museums are filled with portraits of the scions of leading families who led fateful charges, sometimes were harmed, sometimes returned to fame and fortune, all of whom did their part. A lot has changed since the days when our political, business, and academic leaders encouraged, even expected, their children to serve, as part of the growing-up process and as something that many American males just did, with the full support of their loved ones.

Today, the number of congressmen and congresswomen who are also veterans is only about one-third what it was a generation ago, in 1969, and the percentage is falling fast.[2] Only slightly more than one percent of members of Congress have a child serving.

This is *not* a Democrat-versus-Republican issue. It is a class issue—small town, religious, and middle-class Democrats or Republicans are more likely to have someone in the military in their extended social group than wealthy partisans of either party living in big cities.

Why don't the elites serve? They probably never even consider it. If asked, some in the opinion-making field might come up with a political reason. However, before Clinton or Bush were elected, before 9/11, and before the war in Afghanistan, the second Iraq war, and the war on terror, and before gays in the military became an issue in reaction to the "don't ask, don't tell" policy, the elites weren't volunteering, let alone encouraging their children to serve. The "reasons" may change, but one thing remains constant: the expectation that military service is for the "other" and never for the most privileged.

Whatever the putative reasons behind the nonservice of privileged Americans, our concern is that the gap between the opinion makers—the cultural, professional, and business elites—and the military is harming us as a country now and may harm us to a far greater extent in the future. The stakes are high: the U.S. military is an arm of American official activity abroad.

More and more Americans see the military as a kind of magic black box—put any desired outcome in, and results come out. Why didn't we simply "secure Iraq" after we invaded? Why wasn't Osama bin Laden captured in Afghanistan "when we had the chance"? How come we didn't "plan better for the war in Iraq"? Why didn't we "stop the genocide in Rwanda"? Why don't we invade the Sudan

---

2. Donald N. Zillman, "Where Have All the Soldiers Gone II: Military Veterans in Congress and the State of Civil-Military Relations," *Maine Law Review* (2006) (publication forthcoming). Seventy percent of Congress were veterans in 1969. Twenty-five percent were veterans in the Congress of 2004.

to "save the people in Darfur"? Did the military "get to New Orleans fast enough" after Hurricane Katrina?

The country needs to debate our military policy wisely. We are not sure America is doing that today. We are certain of the fact that fewer and fewer civilian leaders and opinion makers have actual military experience, let alone a personal stake in our country's military decisions, a "stake" that stares back at them from their beloved child's boot camp graduation photograph.

We believe we are shortchanging ourselves as a country, and we are shortchanging a generation of smart, motivated Americans who have been prejudiced against service by parents and teachers. Their parents may think they are protecting their children. Their teachers may think they are enlightening them. But perhaps what these young people are being protected from is maturity, selflessness, and the kind of ownership of their country that can give it a better future.

1. It's Personal

★ ★ ★ ★ ★ ★

The evidence is that those who serve and those who don't are looking at each other with growing uneasiness and across a widening philosophical, ideological, political, and even religious social gap.

Frank and Kathy

We were the last people who expected to be drafted into the military. People like us—Frank, a novelist, Kathy, a lawyer with political connections—never would be, we thought. Yet here we are. The last draft in America is a draft of the heart—it takes women and men, it takes parents and grandparents. Someone we love is in the military, and before we know it—sometimes against our will—we, too, are part of the military family.

Of course, like the professional military, this "family draft" doesn't take many people from our demographic. The extended military family, like those in uniform, increasingly includes fewer and fewer of those who are particularly influential in affecting the opinions and policies of the country.

It was not always this way.

During World War I, World War II, and the Cold War, we had conscription, and many people from the influential classes served, either through the draft or by volunteering. About half of the graduating classes of Princeton and Harvard entered the service for a tour of duty in the fifties. Today, less than one percent do.

The change has everything to do with the Vietnam War. After the Vietnam War, America made what turned out to be an almost universally popular decision to create an all-volunteer military. For the first time in history, the country had a large military, wars, and no conscription. It seemed like a perfect solution to our problems of domestic disputes over the use of our military and the blowback from the draft. If you wanted to join, fine. If you didn't, that was fine too. Military service became just another item on an ever-lengthening list of personal choices. And how connected you wanted to be to your country's foreign policy entanglements was optional. If you wanted to live as if the world ended at our borders, that was fine, and if you wanted to take personal responsibility for your citizenship, that was fine too. To use the vernacular of the time you could "do your own thing."

As a result, it has become increasingly comfortable for most young adults of all social classes to avoid even thinking about military service. This nonservice is a reflection of the idea that service is just a choice in the same category as deciding which college to go to, what car to buy, where to go to church or not to go. Those with "better options" simply choose not to join the military.

We believe that the increasing gap between the most privileged classes and those in the military raises three major problems: It hurts our country, particularly our ability to make the best policy possible. It undermines the strength of our civilian leadership, which no longer has significant numbers of members who have the experience and wisdom that comes from national service. Finally, it makes our military less strong in the long run.

And then there is also an intangible, something as real as it is hard to prove: the sense of lost community and the threat to democracy that results when a society accepts a situation that is inherently unfair. When those who benefit most from living in a country contribute the least to its defense and those who benefit less are asked to pay the ultimate price, something happens to the soul of that country. It may be legal, but is it right?

Kathy

I've had a lucky life, even a glamorous one at times, so that in today's culture nothing would predict I would be at home on a military base. I was raised in an upper-middle-class neighborhood where a high-achieving Jewish child could grow up to be anything he or she wanted to be: a doctor *or* a lawyer. Shaker Heights, Ohio, as I knew it, was an earnest place, proud of its SAT scores and the racial and religious diversity of its professional families. The civics lessons that loomed largest in the minds of the class of '82 were the Holocaust, the civil rights movement, Vietnam, and Watergate. The moral of these seemed to be that one should distrust authority figures and find and act on an internal moral compass—not a lesson that leads people to serve their country through a tour of military duty.

After high school I entered the little utopia that is Bryn Mawr College. There I discovered feminism and parlayed my tiny high school leadership experience (running a previously defunct literary magazine) into starting a women's group. We did things like organize issues seminars and rallies to support women's health clinics. At various times in my "activist career" I was arrested for protesting nuclear weapons at an Army base and for civil disobedience at the South African embassy. These were all such scripted and risk-free affairs that my mother, a schoolteacher in town to visit me at the time of the demonstration, decided to join me in the paddy wagon after singing "We Shall Overcome" illegally on the South African embassy's lawn.

I also launched what turned out to be my political career. I met members of Walter Mondale's staff when Mondale was running for president in 1984 and made enough of a nuisance of myself that they let me come out on the road with them. I did advance work for Mondale and Geraldine Ferraro, and have done advance work for every presidential election since then, ending only in 2004.

Advance work led me to fall in love with my country—you get to travel to big cities, small towns, rural farms, inner cities. You put together events to showcase local initiatives that your candidate likes or to spotlight individual people's situations—family farms, AIDS support groups, after-school programs. It really is a big, beautiful country, filled with many sincere people trying to make things better.

I became patriotic along the way and loved the flag I would place in the cutaway shot at a rally. In the meantime, because of the Democrats' talent for losing, I had plenty of time for other activities. I got a graduate policy degree with a focus on international affairs from the Woodrow Wilson School at Princeton University. There, at age twenty-five, I encountered the first military people I knew by name—people who were Army fellows at the school. I found them exotic and extremely well prepared for class. The WWS was a fantastic program; nonetheless, I managed to graduate without knowing we had four different military services (in three branches) or what the differences were between officers and men and women serving enlistments. I went on to work in the progressive foundation world in Manhattan, then in January 1992 started to help out with the campaign of a charismatic young governor from Arkansas.

Working for William Jefferson Clinton was an enormous privilege. I wasn't the first or last to notice President Clinton's staggering intellect and his boundless ability to care about people. He was also considerate and generous to his staff, even to the minor players such as me.

My work for Bill Clinton afforded me one of the greatest thrills a citizen in a democracy can have: the sense of enfranchisement that comes from having helped to elect a president. January 20, 1993, was a magical day for me. I rode in a trailing car in the presidential motorcade from the inauguration at the Capitol, past the cheering crowds on Pennsylvania Avenue, to our first moments in the White House, where we wandered around without guides, poking our heads into offices: *Look, it's the White House Mess! Look, it's the Oval Office!*

The job of doing advance work lets you be a fly on the wall at major happenings. As the person who leads the president through various domestic and foreign visits or sites, the advance person is present at history. Among the most striking experiences for me were those in the just-opened former Soviet Union. I walked through Stalin's dacha (country house), preserved as it had been fifty years ago in the immediate aftermath of his death, the curtains still reeking of cigars. It is closed to visits by the public and stands as an eerie testament to insanity and evil. I walked the woods in Belarus, guided by a KGB director with gold teeth to a clearing where the Soviets ordered the massacre and burial of tens of thousands of intellectuals. I came to understand that the college newspaper columns I wrote mocking Reagan for using the phrase "evil empire" were naïve.

A generation and class of us had been raised to believe that misunderstanding and poverty are the only real-world problems. That is no longer my view. I believe in evil now, borne of either individual illness or Hobbesian reality. I also believe that the propensity to evil requires us to be vigilant.

My time at the White House opened my eyes to the role of the U.S. military in the world. It also brought me in contact with more military people than ever before. At the White House the military was everywhere. Members of the military were in the National Security Council, of course. They ran White House Communications; there were military aides to the president and military people were

White House Fellows. The Navy ran the Mess, the Army drove the cars, the Air Force had the plane, and the Marine Corps flew the helicopters.

The military people we knew were so impressive—tall and direct, knowledgeable about their jobs, dedicated. A lingering question was why they didn't leave the service and get a job in the larger society that would pay them more money and give them a "better" life. But from the president on down there was enormous respect. In fact, the unsolicited handwritten note President Clinton wrote to Frank Schaeffer after he read one of Frank's *Washington Post* editorials seems entirely consistent with what I had seen:

> January 4, 2003
> Dear Frank,
>   One of the greatest joys of the presidency for me was commanding young women and men like your son from many races, religions, and backgrounds. Our country is in good hands as long as it has people like John and his father.
> Sincerely,
> Bill Clinton

After serving in the White House, I went on to work for a billionaire, living in Manhattan near Gracie Mansion with a view of the East River. So there I was: former agitator, feminist, Ivy Leaguer, Clintonite, now an Upper East Sider with a car service and an expense account. Not your usual future "Marine wife" material, I would have thought then. But I had not counted on falling in love with "my" Marine.

Even after I married my husband, I still failed to see myself in terms of the military. I was in love with a man who happened to be a Marine. My husband has a job—what of it? I thought. All of my friends' husbands also have jobs—what difference does it make what that job is? (I will pause for a minute now to allow the experienced military wives who are reading this book to pick themselves up off the floor and stop laughing.) Eventually I did become a military wife, the way a frog in a bath that is slowly turned up to boiling gets cooked: without noticing it.

By the time I was married I was back in D.C. with a political appointment to the Pentagon. I had sought out the Department of Defense position because it matched my interest in international affairs and gave me an opportunity to get to know my husband's "world." That's how we talked. I had my world, the world of political appointees, Council on Foreign Relations meetings, and Ivy League alumni groups—cocktail parties stocked by fancy caterers where my friends and I all plotted our next, more exciting job. And my husband had his world. His seemed to include an awful lot of acronyms.

The Pentagon job turned out to be a great choice, and my boss, John Goodman, taught me a great deal. I came to understand the staggering range of what the Department of Defense (DOD) does. I was also increasingly impressed by the work that military people do—the contingency planning for an array of possible world events, the humanitarian and peacekeeping actions of the mid-'90s, and the many missions that were essentially diplomatic, interacting with governments in every sector of the world. It struck me then that much of real-world action is done by the military. I could see that in the same way a previous generation had gone into the State Department to be a part of history, the current generation could best effect history on a personal level by being in the military. Yet the "best and the brightest," at least the ones I knew, never even considered it.

My daughter was born a year into my marriage, and a few months later we moved to Okinawa, Japan. This was the first shock of my married life. It was a difficult time for me, leaving my career, my friends, my known world of the New York–D.C. corridor. My first

Green Acres experience, I called it, summoning the words of the theme song: "You are my wife—" "—Good-bye, city life!"

It was also my first experience of not being the sole architect of my destiny. I was isolated, living in town with only a few pathetic words of Japanese in my pocket. The truth is, though, it was probably harder for me to learn to be a mother than to be a Marine Corps wife. It took me a good year and a half to settle into motherhood, to be comfortable with the awesome responsibility of raising a human being. It was my mommy boot camp: I was torn down, but built back up again.

The year in Japan was a good year too. My sister joined me; I made good friends and traveled a bit in Asia. I taught a university course on American government and did an unpaid stint as a pundit on a cable TV show. I even went to Tokyo to help advance a presidential trip there, seven-month-old in tow. I have some cute pictures of my baby with President Clinton to show for it.

After Okinawa, we moved to San Diego, where I went to law school (my destiny having caught up with me), and my husband soon deployed. For me, this first deployment was relatively untraumatic— I had one very well-behaved child, and I flew out to rendezvous with my husband twice during his six-month absence, once in Hong Kong and once in Thailand, getting some good shopping in along the way. The thought of a six-month separation had sounded inhumane to me, but I found that my husband and I stayed close through e-mail, having what sometimes seemed like more intimate conversations than we might have during the press of daily life.

I still didn't interact with the other Marine wives that much. I had law school, my child, friends and family nearby. More, I imagined myself different from other officers' wives—old to have a small child, strange to be doing something like school (although part-time) with a young child. It would chafe a bit to hear people enumerate the benefits of being a Marine wife—for instance, "You get to do a lot of traveling." I always wanted to say, "Well, as a matter of fact, I got myself around just fine on my own, thank you very much!" I think I still wasn't comfortable in my skin and was a little prickly, a little defensive. At the same time, I was increasingly impressed with the work my husband did, how much it affected the world. And it continued to strike me how little "my world" knew about it.

On 9/11, I spent the day holding my three-year-old and listening to NPR, wondering where my husband was. Friends who previously hinted that he should probably find responsible work in the civilian world were now suddenly glad to have him in the Marine Corps, and called occasionally for advice (along the lines of: "Should we cancel our vacation to Bali?").

In November of 2002, I had had another baby, and Greg deployed again. By this time I was of course aware of what Marines do. I could picture them in Kuwait—jogging in 100-degree weather wearing gas masks, wary of occasional sniper fire—while I graduated law school and began to study for the bar. I began to realize that this "Marine thing" was not just another job.

On March 19, 2003, as the Marines crossed into Iraq, carrying their effects in 150-pound backpacks, fully expecting a chemical attack, I felt speechless at the bravery of all the Marines I knew. It was typical for us to lose communication with our Marines for terrifying days or even weeks at a time. I was glued to Fox News and CNN until I realized the folly and uselessness of watching these reports when you have someone in country.

The Marines did something unprecedented in that war, covering five hundred miles of an inland invasion in a few weeks. I knew what a real accomplishment that was, and it bothered me to hear people shrug off the military victory: "Well, *of course* our military won so quickly; they far outgun any military in the world." As if that made the task trivial.

Here is an interesting thing I learned about being a military wife. Terribly important people count on you. Those people are your children and your husband. As a parent, you learn quickly that your children understand the world through your eyes—if you find something scary, it will be scary to them. As a military wife, you can't let your children know you are scared about Daddy. They need to feel that Daddy is safe. You are their only means of feeling that way. Your husband needs you too, so he can concentrate on his job. Sometimes it's easier to find strength when you know other people need you; I think military wives (and no doubt the husbands of military women) learn this.

I used to worry about how I could keep the threads of a career together as a military wife. As it turns out, I've found it works well as long as I stay flexible and don't need a lot of the trappings (or money) of a traditional work life. I telecommute to the part-time work I do, legal, writing, or political. During the Kerry campaign, I would take part in meetings via cell phone while leading my toddler around the base stables on a pony. While writing this book, Frank and I have talked daily on the phone and swapped many drafts via e-mail.

My husband deployed for his second tour of duty in Iraq in February 2005. We went into this second experience of war much more seasoned, more confident. For myself, I had a new sense of faith that was very sustaining. The role faith plays in the military, as opposed to in civilian life (particularly among the privileged percentile), is one of the striking differences between the two groups.

While we were in D.C., my husband attended a commanders' course, a curriculum designed to help prepare lieutenant colonels to take their first command. It comes with a companion course for spouses officially called the "Spouses Workshop." My friends and I giggled at the idea of what we called "Commanding Officer Wives School" and what it might cover. It sounded like something out of a Molière play, and more than one person imagined lessons on tea pouring.

In Commanding Officer Wives School you learn how to help make a unit cohesive, how to support very young wives who may be far from home. Perhaps the main theme is how to take care of each other. You learn about death notifications. What the protocol is. How someone is selected as a casualty assistance officer—that is, the person who notifies the family of serious injury or death, and advises them through the ensuing weeks. A current commanding officer wife discussed what happened in her squadron when one of their Marines died in Iraq, how they tried to support the family. The facilitator points out that if you, the commander's wife, write a note or attend the funeral, the family may appreciate it. I think it's safe to say this is information that doesn't lend itself to satire.

Frank

I've lived in a hurry while on a very me-centered quest for fulfillment. I've done most things in life too soon, except for becoming a fiction writer, which I did a little late (publishing my first novel, *Portofino,* when I was thirty-nine), and having John when I was twenty-eight.

In 1970, Genie and I married when we were teenagers. Our first two children, Jessica and Francis, were born when I was more or less still a child. I love Genie even more now than I did the day I met her and was stunned by her beauty. And inexplicably she loves me. Our children grew up and forgave my parental ineptitude. It's called undeserved grace.

My late teens and early twenties—the age when those who volunteer to serve sweat through boot camp and learn to work with others—were spent in artistic pursuits as a somewhat coddled protégé. My patron was Lady Edward Montague (my version of the rich old lady who gave Babar her purse). Back in 1970, Lady Montague was living in the Barbizon Plaza Hotel in New York, and she introduced me to her friend who owned the now defunct Frisch

Gallery, as well as to her society pals, including David Rockefeller's wife, who showed up and bought my first painting sold at my first show.

I enjoyed some early success with shows in New York, Geneva, and London. Then I moved from painting to movie making. I worked in the movie business for about twenty years, as a director and producer. I was following the lure of easy, or at least easier, money, not art. It was a dumb choice because my paintings were pretty good and some of the movies I made were pretty awful. I only partially repaired this folly by getting out of the movie business and back to trying to create something worthwhile when I began to write.

I guess you could call me a bohemian "sixties' type," though with a twist, since my late father, Francis Schaeffer, was a famous American evangelical Protestant theologian who founded a retreat center in Switzerland, where I spent my childhood. So when I left my evangelical background—and Europe—to plunge into the art world, then the feature movie business, and later became a novelist, there was a whiff of rebellion about my choices.

Fast-forward to the summer of 1999: My youngest son, John, was about to ship off to boot camp on Parris Island. By then my second novel had been published and I was writing a third. My two older children were grown. My son Francis was teaching nearby, and Jessica was living in Finland with her film-score-composer/jazz-pianist husband and their two children. I was sitting on a bank of the Merrimack River north of Boston in the big old 1835 brick house Genie and I have lived in since 1980. But I wasn't enjoying the summer. I was brooding mightily. To hell with my tomato patch! To hell with my roses and even the peach tree, and as for writing—forget that! I was watching my last precious weeks with John slip away. And he was headed into the Marines! He might as well have been going to another planet. And who knew how "they" would change him?

I felt as if I were running away from some impending doom, sort of the way I felt one winter night at about two AM, back in 1966, when I was fifteen and ran away from the private British boarding school my parents had put me in. I made it from North Wales to London in the middle of the night by hiding in the toilet of a train for five hours, then spent a week living on the streets before I was caught and returned to my horrified parents. It was the end of my formal education. Beginning with that adventure and continuing through early parenthood and the scramble of artistic self-employment, I was left feeling as if I'd been living on black coffee—twitchy, paranoid, and anxious for the better part of my "grown-up" life. My anxiety level has usually been caused by my own stunts. This time the "stunt" was being pulled by my youngest child. . . .

If you know zip about the military, nothing will make you more anxious than having a son who inexplicably wants to volunteer. My two oldest children did what was expected: private high school followed by NYU for Jessica and Georgetown for Francis. John was our baby. He didn't want to go to college, not right out of high school anyway. He said he was talking to Marine recruiters.

To say I had indulged John would be an understatement. He has been my poem, the tall son of a short father. "Love" is too small a word for the feeling that sucked the air out of my chest when I patted my little boy to sleep. With the older two I learned just how fast children grow up and how the stages fly past. I was determined to enjoy each moment of John's childhood and I did. I was a fixture on the sidelines of every sport he played. I might well have been some ubiquitous weed grown up in the night at countless soccer fields. And I cheered louder than the rowdiest eighth-graders, drawing disapproving looks from other parents as my son led the team to basketball victory after victory.

Why had I not been able to instill a proper reverence for school, college, and career in John? (Okay, I had dropped out and run away, and changed careers, but somehow I'd gotten Jessica and Francis to do what I told them!) Like many of my 1960s' former-hippie-now-yuppie friends, when it came to my own children I wanted them to follow a very predictable upper-middle-class path: top college, good grades, smart jobs, wife/husband, Subaru/Volvo, membership at the Metropolitan Museum of Art, IRA started early, kids, college fund . . . How had I failed my son so badly?

I had become more conservative than some of my friends in the movie and book-writing businesses. Anyway, my enthusiasms for the likes of John McCain made me feel like a "hawk" compared to my left-of-Trotsky friends in Boston, New York's Upper West Side, or L.A. That was until it was *my* son who planned to join! While it was someone else's kid playing the role of spear point of American policy, I could theorize and pontificate with the best of them. But not when it was *my* kid! And this was *before* 9/11, *before* the wars in Afghanistan and Iraq, when service seemed like a peacetime lark.

Genie was far calmer than I was. She always is. Without her steady love and compassion bridging the gap between my views and John's decision, our family might have been torn apart. Genie took the generous and optimistic view.

"He needs to find his way," she said. "Trust John. There is good stuff in him. This isn't the end of the world."

I had been proud of the academic successes of my older children. I liked it when they did things that made it seem as if our family was finally fitting in someplace, even when that place was the North Shore of Boston, an area filled with tweedy people living stodgy circular lives in the shadow of Harvard, the kind of lives I poked fun at.

I never imagined that any of my children would do something insanely self-destructive. Other parents had children who did that. Maybe they hadn't gone to enough of their kids' soccer matches. Maybe they let their babies cry too long at bedtime. I was the cool dad, John's buddy. Why wouldn't he do what I wanted? If I'd been God the Father, I'd never have sent my son to die for anyone.

I felt ashamed of feeling embarrassed by the fact that John was not in college. When my neighbors, people who went to Harvard and drove Saabs, asked about where John was in school, I mentioned that Francis, my "other son," got the top academic award at the Georgetown School of Foreign Service. "My daughter is living in Scandinavia *and* doing graduate studies *and* raising two children *and* speaks three languages *and* is running a successful ceramics business . . ."

I felt like Judas. Nevertheless I let everyone know John could have gone anywhere and that he "chose the Marines as a poet chooses to forgo painkillers after surgery, in order to taste the pain so he can write about it later." I came up with all sorts of bullshit like that. "He wants to live large," I lamely said.

Then I began to get John's boot camp letters.

I began to see him grow, to see the desperate isolation and disorientation of the first weeks give way to a new confidence. And I wanted to stay connected to my beloved son, so I began to read about the Marines. I also began to meet former Marines who had been invisible to me before. I started noticing all those eagle, globe, and anchor lapel pins.

Where had I been all my life? In my heart I started to understand that it was degrading to have to justify John's being a Marine to people who struck me as snobs, in other words, to people like me, people who never lifted a finger for anybody. We didn't "do" selfless. We were selfish. It began to occur to me that maybe something was wrong with me and not with John.

John's letters moved me. So did the people I met after I put a Marines bumper sticker on my car. I found that I'd stumbled into a brotherhood by proxy, that people with tears of pride in their eyes, total strangers, would tell me about a son or daughter in the military.

I found that leaders in my community, men from another generation, when serving our country was a normal rite of passage, came
up to me and congratulated me for having a son in the military.
They would sometimes tell me their life stories; tell me something
they had never mentioned before about fighting on Okinawa, or at
the Chosin Reservoir in Korea, or about coming home to a spiteful
reception after fighting in Vietnam, or about the friend they lost in
Beirut.

John graduated boot camp in the late fall of 1999. He headed
out to his MOS (military occupational specialty school) training in
his chosen specialty, signals intelligence. (He had originally signed
up for four years but agreed—when asked—to serve a fifth year so
he could get the training he needed for his job.) He spent over a
year training and waiting for his top-secret security clearance. Then
came 9/11.

I knew our lives had changed forever as soon as I saw the second
plane hit. I knew that John would go to war. I knew I was not strong
enough to endure this alone. I began to depend on my new military
family. And I began to worry about other people's sons and daughters almost as much as I was worrying about mine.

I have never been as frightened or as proud as I was on September 14, when John and I were finally able to get in touch on the
phone. From a base in Florida he calmly told me he was ready and
willing to fight for our country, to be part of the counterattack and
defense.

This is what I wrote in my diary as John was deployed to war a
few months later:

I'd write John a letter to take along, but I don't want to scare
him. He knows the depth of my love. I have this impulse to
review our lives, to hold forth, give him a last lecture on all
that is important to me. But I don't. In the face of his sacrifice

absolute honesty is demanded. And the truth is that over the years much of what I've said to my children is somewhat of a lie. I've pretended to be much more certain of my beliefs than I really am.

As a father it's been my job to present a world of order, right and wrong, and faith to my children. I have tried to push back the chaos, give them shelter to grow in. But now, on the cusp of this great divide that is about to separate John and me, I can't play father any longer. I can only say what I really know, that I love my son and am begging God to watch over him, even though I lack the faith to always believe that God is even there. I cling to the hope.

A door is closing. The traditional father-son roles are about to reverse. I'm staying safe at home. My child is about to risk his life to protect me. I am powerless to help him. He is the man now and I'm the frightened child.

By the summer of 2004, as the five years of John's service began to wind down, I had come to understand my own achievements (real or imagined) in an altogether new light. Every loving father wants to have a child surpass him, do better than he has. I had always thought of this in material or career terms. Now I realized that it had happened in moral and character terms. I was deeply proud of my daughter, Jessica, her career, her choice of a wonderful husband, her two lovely children, and her common sense and ongoing academic accomplishments. And my son Francis is a brilliant, selfless schoolteacher and the kind of absolutely dependable friend I call at all hours just to talk. I am immensely proud of him. But John's service threw my life into sharp perspective in a new way. My Marine had stood up for us all when it counted. He had done his job when his country needed him. He had connected our family to our country in a deep way.

In some ways John had become more in five years than I have in a lifetime. You could see it from the way he walked into a room. You could see it in how people related to him. I could see the change in the way he aced his application to one of the most prestigious universities in America, even having been out of the academic loop for five years and at war, even having heartily disliked school from kindergarten on.

And he has done very well. "It's not too hard, Dad," from the son who never did his homework. "You do what needs to be done, study, get the paper written, whatever it takes. Compared to working shifts where if you screw up people die, school isn't so hard."

My son has become the sort of man I've always liked best, a member of the so-called greatest generation, though "his" war wasn't the Second World War but the ambiguously misnamed War on Terror. Nevertheless my son has become that sort of steady, self-confident, self-deprecating, all-round good guy I've admired. He seems effortlessly comfortable in his own skin. I had assumed that those sorts of people just didn't get made anymore, that it was a generational thing. I was wrong. "They" still do make men and women of character and inner strength. They make them in the United States military. They do it every day.

Slowly it had dawned on me: John joining the military was the best thing he could have done. And it was one of the best things that had happened to our family. It put us through anguish. But then everything worthwhile in life is hard.

Frank and Kathy

At any given moment Americans of all political persuasions are calling for the United States to intervene in world affairs. Liberals and conservatives may differ on where our military should be used, but both camps call for it to be deployed on a regular basis to stop genocide, fight terror, provide humanitarian relief, end ethnic cleansing, spread democracy, interdict drug traffic, rescue American civilians from danger, and yes, undo foreign policy messes of our own making from time to time. The list is as endless as the number of American political leaders with causes.

Before our family members were in the military, we would not have cared much about how it was portrayed or used or abused. Now we do. We are not approaching this subject "academically," though we do believe that we have backed up what we are saying with facts and by pointing to serious studies done by others. But we are not pretending that the issue of who serves or does not serve in our military is not personal.

2. "Not for People Like Us": Or How the Privileged See the Military

★★★★★★★★★★★★★★★★★★★★

"I've raised my sons to be sensitive to others, and to be critical thinkers, so I don't think they'd be well suited for the military."

—Los Angeles doctor and mother

Kathy and Frank

How can we argue that there is a disconnect between people of privilege and the military, when the military is so often widely praised? After all, "Support Our Troops" magnetic ribbons adorn the sides of many Lexuses and Mercedeses as well as pickup trucks. Indeed, since the late nineties, all major polls have shown the military to be the most trusted American institution—ahead of Congress, the media, even churches.[1] It has become a mantra for virtually all of us—including our top leadership—the claim to be

---

1. David C. King and Zachary Karabell, *The Generation of Trust: How the U.S. Military Has Regained the Public's Confidence Since Vietnam* (Washington, DC: American Enterprise Institute Press 2003) pp. 1–6.

"proud of the men and women who serve in the military."[2] Even antiwar groups and pacifists routinely pay homage to "our men and women."

Privileged folks may be proud of the troops, but most contemporary men and women in uniform are strangers to the most influential segment of society. Mark Shields, syndicated columnist, former Marine, and PBS pundit, noted in a recent essay on this subject that "probably nobody at any Washington dinner party tonight—liberal or conservative, Bush appointee or Democratic holdover—personally knows any enlisted man or woman now defending the nation."[3]

Not too long ago the sons of presidents, bankers, and oilmen regularly served. This was even true for members of powerful dynasties such as the Roosevelts, the Kennedys, the Sulzbergers (owners and publishers of the *New York Times*), and the Bushes. Now, however, not one grandchild from those powerful dynasties serves.

The last president with a child (or son-in-law) in uniform was Lyndon Johnson. Prior to Johnson, it was common for a president's son to be in or have seen service. And it wasn't only public servants who shared the responsibility—movie stars and professional athletes joined the ranks when asked. It was considered the right thing to do, somewhat along the lines of the biblical adage that of those to whom much has been given much will be required.

Though post-Vietnam it is common for people in positions of influence to publicly praise the people who serve, there is evidence that of all segments of society, the leadership class has the least esteem

---

2. *Soldiers and Civilians: The Civil-Military Gap and American National Security,* ed. Peter D. Feaver and Richard H. Kohn (Cambridge, MA: MIT Press, 2001); hereafter *Soldiers and Civilians*.

3. Mark Shields, "In Power, but Not in Peril," *United We Serve,* ed. E. J. Dionne, Kayla Meltzer Drogosz, and Robert E. Litan (Washington, D.C.: Brookings Institution Press, 2004) p. 135.

for the military. Perhaps this is because of all Americans they have the fewest personal connections to the military.

In the most important recent study on the subject of civil-military affairs, American leaders and members of the general public who had no military service experience were polled, along with military and reserve leaders, and civilian veterans.[4] As expected, virtually everyone repeated that they were "proud of the men and women who serve in the military" and have "confidence in the ability of our military to perform well in wartime." But our society's most powerful leaders who had no military experience parted company with other American groups in significant ways.[5] For instance, fewer than *half* of the leaders in the larger society thought the U.S. armed forces were attracting high-quality, motivated recruits. In contrast, a strong majority—more than three-quarters—of military leaders thought that they were.[6]

People in leadership positions in society and without military experience, in fact, had the lowest opinion of the military of any group surveyed. While a majority of all other groups said they had a "great deal" of confidence in the military, only about a third of those in the elite classes said the same.[7] Civilians in the leadership class—in other words, our most privileged citizens—judged that

---

4. Peter D. Feaver and Richard H. Kohn, principal investigators, Project on the Gap between the Military and American Society, Triangle Institute of Security Studies (TISS), Durham, N.C., 1998–2001; hereafter cited as TISS.

5. Ole R. Holsti, "Of Chasms and Convergences: Attitudes and Beliefs of Civilians and Military Elites at the Start of the New Millennium," in *Soldiers and Civilians,* table 1.23, p. 72, "Opinions about the U.S. Military: Responses in the 1998–1999 Survey." Interestingly, while virtually all military strongly agreed they were proud of the people who served, only about half of the elite nonveterans strongly agreed with the statement. The rest agreed somewhat.

6. TISS, Ibid. Still, interestingly perhaps, virtually all the military folks strongly agreed with this statement.

7. TISS, table 1.17, p. 61.

military culture was very rigid, not at all creative, and not particularly honest.[8] These opinions were in marked contrast to the military's view of itself and to the much higher esteem the military was held in by those in the less privileged classes from which more military people are currently drawn.[9]

Members of the military are strangers to the upper classes. And it seems privileged folks want to keep it that way. They have consciously or unconsciously done all they can to avoid having anyone close to them become a member of the military. Private high schools and many of our leading colleges are hostile to military recruiters or have banned them and organizations like the ROTC (or JROTC) altogether from their campuses. And speaking anecdotally, the majority of the people we have run across who are not connected to the military already, who are making good money or are involved in opinion making or in academia, the media or in policy work, flinch at the suggestion that their children serve.

One way to sum up the disconnect between the wealthiest and most influential class of Americans and our military is to ask yourself this question: Would you be surprised to hear that actor Leonardo DiCaprio or Steven Spielberg's son or the daughter of the president of Yale or one of George Bush's daughters or a Kennedy grandchild or the son of the president of Microsoft had enlisted? If the answer is yes, then why would you be surprised? What assumptions have you made about our all-volunteer forces and who is the "appropriate" volunteer?

Research backs the intuitive assumption that our elites just don't want their children to serve these days. In the survey above, leaders

8. TISS, table 1.16, p. 60. Seventy-eight point six percent of civilian nonveteran leaders identify military culture as rigid. Fifteen percent see it as creative. Fifty-eight percent think it's honest.
9. Ibid. The figures are, 51.5 percent see it as rigid, 43.5 percent see it as creative, 94.4 percent see it as honest.

in the larger society were four or five times more likely than a military leader to say that they would be "disappointed if a child of mine joined the military."[10]

Frank

Had I been polled in 1999 (when John signed up), I would have marked myself in that "disappointed" group too. When my son graduated from high school, I felt as singled out and embarrassed as I had when I was a child and my mother would say excruciatingly long graces over our meals in public. The rest of the world tucked into their rosemary chicken while we "witnessed to the lost," over plates of congealing food. I spent the better part of an early chapter in my semiautobiographical novel, *Portofino,* describing in detail what it was like to furtively watch other diners furtively watching us, sitting with our heads bowed while Mom delivered her loud long nightly and highly personal monologue to God.

That's a little bit how I felt when John announced from the podium of his private school at graduation that he was going into the Marines—mortified. I had known he was going to do it, but when he spoke the words in public, it still came as a shock. Everyone else had named a top college. Other parents would not look in our direction. The applause was a trifle polite and seemed nervous. John stood there so tall and so beautiful in his gown. The emerald lawn was extra green and perfect-looking, framed by the snappy yellow-and-white-striped tent pavilion. Well-dressed parents ferried the prizes their sons and daughters had won from the pavilion back to their Mercedeses, Saabs, and Jags. John had his prizes too, for writing and athletics. But they seemed wasted. What was the use of being one of the school's best poets—someone who had been invited to read along with adults at local libraries—when he

---

10. TISS, Table 1.23, p. 73.

was going to throw away his talents and join the Marines? What was the point of John having been a great athlete when all he would use his beautiful body for now was to crawl around in the mud with God knows what kind of riffraff, instead of winning the track scholarship that everyone had assumed he'd pick up as he sailed into college?

Champagne flowed for parents and fruit drinks for the students. The other parents and kids all looked so safe and content. They looked well and happy and rich, beyond the slings and arrows of ordinary life, as if they had figured out some way to live forever. I tried to picture John in boot camp. I couldn't. I had a much easier time imagining him in a flag-draped coffin. Why should John be any different from all his friends? Why is life unfair?

"What a waste," commented a parent seated near me at John's graduation.

"We should carefully evaluate what went wrong," said another parent, a professor of history at Brown University, at a postgraduation parents' day encounter with the headmaster.

Kathy

I cross between the worlds of opinion makers and the military when I drive back and forth between Washington, D.C., and Jacksonville, North Carolina. D.C. is career strategizing over great food, listening to my friends' nanny-crises, admiring real art on people's walls, and going to meetings about how to fix the Democratic Party. Jacksonville is fixing spaghetti dinners on paper plates, going to volunteer meetings in rooms full of linoleum and metal folding furniture, relying on my neighbors to watch the kids when I'm desperate, and staying up late at night to pack cardboard boxes with children's artwork, almonds, old *New Yorker*s, and love notes.

Many of my lifelong friends are in Washington. I care about the business there, and I am still idealistic about it (although it helps sometimes to be a bit removed from the sausage-making aspect of politics). But some of the people I run across in the Capitol see the military as if through the small end of the telescope, and I have to summon the energy to address the issues that come up.

From the earliest days of my marriage, people said little things, questions probing how it could happen that someone like my husband—so smart, so versatile—ended up in the military. Was there a tragedy in his past, perhaps? Other military folks from nonmilitary backgrounds usually have experiences like these. The mother of a Marine officer I know once said about him, about nine years into his career, "What a waste of a college education." (This man now has several advanced degrees, has taught at MIT, and is in command of one of the air groups operating in Iraq.)

Said one mother to me, "I've raised my sons to be sensitive to others, and to be critical thinkers, so I don't think they'd be well suited for the military." *Critical thinking* is of course the byword of liberal arts education, and the military is the imagined antithesis of it, where one merely, unthinkingly, follows orders.

A young friend of mine, now an attorney making many times a general officer's salary at a top Manhattan law firm, recounted to me how he had once wanted to join the military for a tour of duty, having picked up an old-fashioned notion somewhere. "It's not for people like us," his family told him. "You're too smart; you've got too much going for you to throw your life away like that."

A vivacious young woman of my acquaintance, a public-interest activist and Stanford grad, dated a Marine recently, much to her own surprise. "It's not popular with my friends," she admits. "They wonder if I'm compromising my ideals."

Kathy and Frank

Writing about the military-civilian disconnect, author Josiah Bunting III finds that students at the top boarding and public high schools and the famous universities and colleges are now "fully settled . . . in their contempt or condescension for the profession of arms."[11] The situation is tantamount to a withdrawal of the privileged intellectual, professional, and commercial classes, their children, or those destined for high position from the active military service of America. As Bunting puts it, few of those who "lead our country, who control its resources and institutions, direct and inflect its tastes and opinions, batten most avidly upon its treasures and most lavishly upon its expensive entertainments" are touched by war or those who serve. And this state of affairs is "dangerous . . . unworthy . . . wrong."

Andrew J. Bacevich, a professor at Boston University and Vietnam veteran, points out that while "minority and working-class kids might serve; the sons and daughters of those who occupy positions of influence in the corporate, intellectual, academic, journalistic, and political worlds have better things to do."[12] He summarized the attitude of those in high position as, "Although we don't know you, rest assured we admire you—now please go away."[13]

RECRUITING

The area that best exposes the deep discomfort that putatively supportive segments of America show toward the military is the reality of military recruiting. After all, logically, if you "support the

---

11. Josiah Bunting III, "Class Warfare," *The American Scholar* 74, no. 1 (Winter 2005) p. 12.

12. Andrew J. Bacevich, *The New American Militarism: How Americans Are Seduced by War* (New York: Oxford University Press, 2005) p. 26.

13. Ibid., p. 29.

troops" and are grateful for the protection they offer, then their act of service is of inestimable value. And if you don't want the draft to be used to maintain our military's numbers, then one would think every courtesy would be extended to recruiters. Moreover, in America many of us like to pretend that we are a classless society. "Equal opportunity" is a mantra for the right, left, rich, and poor. But when it comes to military service, the upper classes don't even pretend they want the playing field level.

Perhaps this is part of a larger shift of our country toward becoming a plutocracy, the "two nations" some politicians have talked about. We've learned to accept the fact that a failed CEO gets a $40-million golden handshake, while the company's workers get nothing. And now we are learning to accept the fact that anyone but the most privileged Americans defend us, and that the most privileged Americans find excuses to make sure their children are not even exposed to recruiters.

Anti-recruiter actions are not limited to a few elite "liberal" universities. There are a growing number of Americans who will not allow their children's high schools to give their names and addresses to recruiters. Under the No Child Left Behind Act, high schools are required to give the names, phone numbers, and addresses of graduating students to military recruiters unless parents request their children be omitted from the program. Many parents apparently find it unbearably onerous that their children might be asked to even consider serving their country, even though their children not only may refuse the phone call but, of course, are under no obligation to join.

In challenging the law, Donna Lieberman, executive director of the New York Civil Liberties Union, argued, "Students have a right to not be bothered by aggressive military recruiters."[14] So not being

---

14. *New York Times,* "Uncle Sam Wants Student Lists, and Schools Fret," January 29, 2003.

asked to even consider service is now defended as some sort of new civil right.[15]

A number of wealthy communities have even tried to launch initiatives to make their towns "recruiting free" zones, where the military is banned. Cambridge, Massachusetts, San Francisco, California, and other well-off enclaves have followed suit. This is a position that has excited some controversy. *Mother Jones,* a left-wing publication published several articles condemning the ability of recruiters to reach high school students. In response, Steven J. Naplan, who served as director for democracy and human rights at the Clinton White House's National Security Council, wrote:[16]

> "Privacy" is the smokescreen behind which *Mother Jones* and these critics attempt to mask their discomfort with the U.S. military—the same military which saved hundreds of thousands of Africans from certain starvation in the early 1990s, saved hundreds of thousands of Bosnian and Kosovar Muslims from mass murder just a few years later, and which today trains the young men and women who risk and sometimes lose their lives to protect us all from the terrorists who would happily take the lives of every last *Mother Jones* editor, writer, and subscriber. . . .
>
> If the U.S. military is to reflect the diversity of America and is to be peopled by the talented, dedicated young Americans we'd want protecting our freedoms and representing our nation, it has no choice but to engage in the extensive recruitment of high school seniors—an honorable and vital mission which deserves our cooperation, not obstruction. In the broadest sense, the U.S. military protects our freedom

15. Ibid.
16. Steven J. Naplan, communication with the authors, November 27, 2002.

to advocate progressive politics. The U.S. military is not the enemy.

The drafters of a local ballot measure in San Francisco apparently don't agree. Their initiative is called "College Not Combat," and it asks city officials and university administrators to exclude military recruiters from both colleges and high schools in San Francisco, even at the cost of forsaking government dollars. It urges the city to create scholarships and training programs to reduce the military's appeal to young adults. A report on the initiative described it as "part of a nationwide movement against the Pentagon's recruiting efforts."[17]

One otherwise pro-military parent was explicit about this point when speaking to recruiters recently. Marine recruiter Staff Sergeant Jason Rivera, twenty-six, went to a home in a well-to-do suburb outside of Pittsburgh to talk to the parents of a high school student who had expressed interest in joining the Marine Corps Reserves. Two American flags flew in the yard. The mother greeted the recruiter wearing an American flag T-shirt. "I want you to know we support you," she gushed. But, explained, as she sent him away, "Military service isn't for our kind of people."[18]

THE POSITION LAID BARE

Frank had a conversation that seems to us to lay bare the not-with-my-privileged-child upper-class thinking in all its splendid confusion.

Rose (not her real name) is the quintessential resident of Boston. She is a Radcliffe graduate, and her husband and only son are Harvard alums. She is wealthy and describes herself as a progressive

---

17. Associated Press, "Initiative Opposes Military Recruiting on Campus," *New York Times,* July 13, 2005.
18. Jack Kelly, "Parent-Trap Snares Military Recruiters," *Jacksonville Daily News,* August 22, 2005, p. 5A.

activist. She sits on the boards of important local and national environmentalist groups. She is the quintessential enlightened WASP's WASP. In her social dealings with Frank, she has been unfailingly kind. However, over the military issue, and especially Frank's son's joining, all Rose's rather polite social sensitivities seemed to have evaporated, at least during one particular conversation.

Frank and Rose were talking about John's military service. Rose launched into a somewhat disjointed monologue. Later, Frank rushed home and wrote it all down, inspired to use the material as the basis of a character in his novel *Baby Jack*. Here is some of what she said:

> "Afghanistan was not all bad; I could rationalize Afghanistan, but there is *nothing* about this war [in Iraq] I can rationalize . . . My father served in World War II. But that was a good war . . .
>
> "Perhaps there is something valuable about military discipline, something like the Native American males did—go camp alone in the woods for two weeks, then you could be a man. But I'd be horrified if *my* son volunteered.
>
> "I don't think all-male societies are dimensional. I think they are one-dimensional. I know they tolerate women in the military these days, but John is in the Marines and they train all those boys together and the females train separately. What does that imply? You must try to get John to reread *On the Beach* and *All Quiet on the Western Front* and *Catch-22* before it is too late . . . You never know, he might *reenlist*! They do brainwash these poor boys, you know!
>
> "Don't misunderstand me. I do know people for whom the military was a constructive experience. There was a former Marine at Harvard Law my husband was in school with, and I believe he is a judge now. However, who wants to kill or be killed? There is no discussion possible. There is no logic.

"You should ask John, What are your needs? What needs propelled you into the military?

"If my son was about to do this, here is what I'd tell him: 'You should aim to work at the cabinet level.' I would say; 'If you want to serve your country, work to develop *real* leadership, to make a *real* difference. Why don't you work on one of those political campaigns?' I'd ask."

We have come to see this conversation as a sort of touchstone summary of all the many conversations we have both had with people who have had no personal contact with anyone in the military. In other words, going to war is, above all, about the self—about individual choice and the individual exercise of conscience; about subconscious, perhaps even unhealthy, needs; and about balancing ambitions and what is in one's own best interest. And all these factors add up to . . . saying no to military service and feeling morally superior for making that choice.

Some public figures in America have spoken about this issue. For instance, Louis Caldera, secretary of the army in the Clinton administration, wonders why calls for national service usually focus on projects such as building housing for poor people and tutoring inner city children, but do not include calls for military service. Caldera speculates that it may come from the "misconceptions about the nature of modern military service, discomfort with the fundamental role of the military, and lingering suspicion and hostility arising from an antiwar movement that spanned three decades, and unhappiness with current policies toward openly gay service members."[19]

---

19. Louis Caldera, "The American Military and the Idea of Service" in *United We Serve*, p. 150.

THE GROWING GAP

The gap between the upper classes and the military reinforces its own existence, a little bit the way racism is reinforced in all-white, segregated communities, where many well-meaning people can say of the "other," "I just don't know any of them." Analysis of why people choose to join the military shows that the single biggest factor is whether someone has a direct personal experience with someone they admire who is in or was in the service. Young men and women who have known and looked up to someone who wore a uniform and spoke positively about the experience are significantly more likely to be interested in joining the military than those who have not.

Frank's son John mentions Matt Snider, an Air Force captain (now a major) he met just a few times and how impressed he was with him, his dedication, and what an all-round inspiring human being he was. And John knew one boy in a nearby town—Max Boucher—who volunteered for the Marines. John had always liked and admired Max. And by coincidence Max's little brother Asher got to Parris Island a few weeks ahead of John. These few casual contacts were enough to make the idea of volunteering tangible.

Kathy's husband, Greg, was influenced in part by his adopted godfather, Pat Fitzsimons, who became a role model and mentor to Greg when he was in college. Pat was Chief of Police in Seattle when Greg met him, a wonderfully ethical, kind, and successful man who had also been a Marine Corps officer.

Several university classmates of Frank's son John showed an interest in military service after getting to know John, none of whom had considered it before. One of his friends actually volunteered. Until they met John, his new friends had never known anyone in the military and had never even considered the possibility of joining. (John is going to a college that banned the ROTC from campus back in the Vietnam era and has never asked them back.) All of a sudden the military had a face, a face they liked. But few upper class children ever meet anyone in the military today.

As a result of dwindling personal contacts with the military, what intelligent, motivated, and idealistic young people are left with are their parents' post-Vietnam biases and fears, the mass media, and what they hear from their often anti-military teachers.

THE UNIVERSITIES

In 1956, 400 out of 750 in Princeton's graduating class went into the military. In contrast, in 2004, 9 members of Princeton's graduating class entered the services, and they *led* the Ivy League in numbers! In 2003, the only student at Columbia planning to become a military officer was such an anomaly she merited a whole story in the *New York Times* headlined, "For a Future Soldier Life on a Liberal Campus Can Be a Battle" (April 2, 2003). In the story, Marine officer candidate Rebekah Pazmino said she felt constantly under attack. According to the area Marine recruiters Frank talked to in a follow up, she eventually felt so harassed she dropped out of the program altogether.

This e-mail to Frank from another student confirms that Ms. Pazmino was no exception.

> I am a twenty-two-year-old college student about to graduate . . . My heart is pulling me toward the Navy. My father was, or rather is, a Marine and he instilled much of the spirit of the Marine Corps in me growing up.
>
> My college experience is a much different matter. I am an anthropologist . . . An extremely liberal educational system and an even more radically liberal anthropological community surrounds me.

In my path toward the Navy, I have been attempting to gather letters of recommendation and have hit a wall. Many of my professors have praised me as an academician but refused to write the recommendations for me on the basis that they are conscientious objectors . . .

The truth of it is all of my school has been hostile toward the military. I have met more resistance in the past two months of exploring the possibility of commissioning than I have ever had to contend with before . . .

Thank you,

(Name withheld)

Charles Moskos conducted a survey of 430 undergraduates in his introduction to sociology class at Northwestern University. A large majority of them had negative impressions of military life, with lifestyle, threat of danger, and length of commitment heading people's lists.[20] This is not a surprising result. It also confirms another study Moskos did. In his sociology classes he conducted studies that demonstrated how lack of personal contact with military men and women often precludes people from even thinking about joining the military, and conversely how personal contact goes a long way toward humanizing and legitimizing the idea of service.

At the university level, some of the outright hostility toward military service, particularly from the faculty, is focused on ROTC. Such top universities as Harvard, Yale, Stanford, University of Chicago, Brown, and Columbia do not even allow ROTC access to campus to present the option of military service and the scholarship to their students. The current stated reason for banning ROTC is the "don't ask, don't tell" law, which prohibits openly gay people from serving.

---

20. Charles Moskos, "Patriotism-Lite Meets the Citizen-Soldier," in *United We Serve*, p. 37.

ROTC's absence on campus does not help to change the law about gays in the military—only Congress could do that, so the protest is misdirected—but it does very effectively discourage some of the country's best students from volunteering for duty or ever meeting someone who has. And no one even pretends to think that if the policy on gays in the military changed, the elite universities would suddenly encourage their students to volunteer.

The divide between those who serve and those who don't now goes far beyond any one battle in America's culture wars. The current antipathy to the military has its roots in the politics of the 1960s and early '70s. And it seems to us another factor has been added: class. The spirit of the student deferments and exemptions of the Vietnam era has been carried forward into the all-volunteer era.

The faculty of many top universities seem to believe that their students are entitled to not be bothered with something like military service. "Our kind" belongs on a faster track. We are reminded of Rose's comment: "You should aim to work at the cabinet level . . . If you want to serve your country, work to develop *real* leadership, to make a *real* difference."

We contend that military service might in fact confer the real-world experience, confidence, and moral authority that no university can offer to its students. Some students who spend a few years between high school and college in the military might actually arrive in college with the discipline and maturity to make better use of the experience.

In short, an anti-military college culture that may once have had political roots in the Vietnam era has now deteriorated into plain elitism and a set of fossilized, unchallenged anti-military assumptions. And once in a while—as with the gays-in-the-military debate—the old bias is updated and given new "reasons." But such updating seems to us to be a sham. For instance, in 2005 Harvard Law School prosecuted a suit to allow it to both ban the military from recruiting its graduates on campus, while still keeping the federal funding that the Solomon amendment requires them to forgo in such circumstances. Stripped bare of the gays-in-the-military political pretense, Harvard Law School's attempt to prevent military recruiters from even asking the school's students to consider service was startlingly elitist. The law school, which is part of an institution that has a $25-billion endowment (at the last count), that disproportionately draws the sons and daughters of the self-perpetuating elite, that pays its financial managers millions of dollars annually, was suing our government to stop its students from *even being asked* to just think about joining the sons and daughters of middle-class and working-class Americans defending all of us.

The sheer hubris implicit in such a shameless act is staggering. And it is hard to see how this NIMBYism (*not in my backyard*; or worse—let-somebody-poor-brown-black-or-rural-white-do-all-the-heavy-lifting) can be dressed up as "progressive." Meanwhile, Harvard Law School encourages recruiting from the bastions of moral probity that represent claimants such as Enron, provide the tobacco industry with lobbyists, or whoever else can pay a $140,000-per-year starting salary to recruit Harvard Law's lucky graduates.

When looking at the recent history of the Ivy League, one doesn't need to look hard to find many examples of how our elites' attitude toward military service has changed. Harvard University had the first ROTC program in the country. Neil Rudenstine, the former president of Harvard, was commissioned through the ROTC program at Princeton in 1956 as an undergraduate and served along with literally hundreds of his classmates. As of 2005, however, three anonymous Harvard alums had to fund the handful of ROTC students on campus to participate in MIT's ROTC program. Harvard's school government is so hostile to ROTC that they forbid any level of support at all. Here are some examples of what happens when Harvard meets military.

Members of Harvard's faculty have reportedly yelled out disparaging remarks to a passing ROTC student in uniform, and students in Harvard Yard asking passersby to sign holiday cards for service members overseas on the Christmas after 9/11 were met by a shout of "fascists."[21] In fact, in 2002 students in Harvard's ROTC program created an organization to seek to encourage "greater tolerance at Harvard for those in uniform." Members of the organization acknowledged that they are "continually disheartened by the persistent anti-ROTC sentiment on Harvard's campus," pointing out poignantly that they, the cadets, have taken an oath to "protect the lives and freedoms of American citizens, even sacrificing our lives if duty calls."[22] The then-outgoing director of the MIT program that included Harvard ROTC students noted in a farewell address that the Harvard Law School "still holds the military with disdain."[23] Harvard University President Lawrence Summers has alienated some of his faculty with his support for ROTC.

On Columbia University's campus, students and faculty have been embroiled in a controversy over ROTC, which has led to many public comments on all sides. Perhaps the most notorious and extreme were statements made by Nicholas Paul De Genova, an assistant professor in the Department of Anthropology/Latino Studies, at a Columbia University "teach-in" protesting the war in Iraq. As reported in the New York Times, Professor De Genova said, "I personally would like to see a million Mogadishus," a reference to the Somali city where, in 1993, American soldiers were ambushed and eighteen killed who were then dragged through the streets. Now,

---

21. Christopher M. Loomis, "Senior to Sail Troubled Waters," Harvard Crimson, June 10, 2004; Charles B. Cromwell, "Explaining the Uniform," Harvard Crimson, February 7, 2002.
22. Ibid.
23. Brian L. Baker, LTC, "A Perspective From the Professor of Military Science," reported in www.AdvocatesForROTC.org, November 30, 2004.

of course we are not arguing that this is a typical response. But consider a few more examples. At a forum on Columbia's campus in 2003, one of the presenters argued against a "military presence in Columbia's student body" because members of the armed forces are trained to "evaporate dissent" and thus would impede free and open debate in the classroom. Another presenter condemned the entire U.S. military as racist.[24] In a column in Columbia's student newspaper, another student charged that ROTC participants want to "rape [gays] with broomsticks." The writer went on to say that joining the military is "flushing your education down the toilet" and that he "cannot comprehend why anyone would want to be in the military."[25]

Many alumni from Columbia and even some students have fought to reinstate ROTC at that campus, but thus far, they have failed. Columbia is not unique in its apparent hostility to our military. Professor David Gelernter describes the climate at Yale:

> Here in academia, my colleagues seem determined to turn American soldiers into an out-of-sight, out-of-mind servant class who are expected to do their duty and keep their mouths shut . . . If you think I'm too hard on my fellow professors, explain to me why Army ROTC host colleges do not include Harvard, Yale, Stanford, the University of Chicago, Caltech . . . (Princeton and a few other top universities deserve credit for not being on this list.)
>
> How can you be terrified of an alleged new draft . . . and opposed to ROTC's soliciting first-rate volunteers?
>
> . . . A few weeks ago, I spoke [in] an informal debate at

---

24. Nat Jacks, "Panel Speakers Link ROTC to War With Iraq," *Columbia Spectator,* April 1, 2003.

25. Nick Rosenthal, "ROTC, You Are (Still) Not Wanted Here," *Columbia Spectator,* February 16, 2005.

Yale, and an imposing middle-aged man with fierce white hair came up afterward to ask me where I got the nerve to support a president who sends young soldiers to their deaths? (Lots of approving nods.)

. . . A 17-year-old boy tried to explain to the white-haired man (in his straightforward, soft-spoken way) that those soldiers had chosen to be where they were; had understood and accepted the dangers; loved life just as much as the man did, but had different ideas about how to live it. The 17-year-old mentioned that he and a friend planned to join the Marines when they finished college.

. . . I had a stake in the argument: the 17-year-old is my son. I don't know whether he'll make it into the Marines; we'll be proud of him either way. I do know that there is a time for every purpose under heaven, and that age 17 is a good time for caring about honor and duty *and* demonstrating the stuff you are made of.[26]

Or take Stanford. In 1956, 1,100 Stanford students enrolled in ROTC; today there are 29. They are trained off-campus, taking military science and national defense courses at Berkeley or Santa Clara, classes for which Stanford University grants them no credit— although the students can get credit on campus for classes in hip-hop or yoga.[27] One Stanford professor contends that training for military service is "fundamentally unacceptable at a university"; another that top schools should not teach "militaristic approaches to problems."[28]

At Brown, ROTC students (like those at most schools) report

26. "Soldiers Do Us the Honor," *Los Angeles Times,* April 15, 2005.
27. Christina Hoff Sommers, "Repressing ROTC," *Washington Post,* August 10, 2003, p. B7.
28. Ibid. Barton Bernstein, professor of history, and Cecilia Ridgeway, sociologist and member of the Stanford Faculty Senate, quoted.

that most other students at least "tolerate" them, but that they do get their "share of harassment." One Brown cadet recounts having to move his seat in class after a student complained that his uniform "makes me feel uncomfortable." Like his Harvard counterpart, this lone cadet pleads with his classmates not to "rush to judgment on a person in uniform, consider that while cadets are united in our . . . desire to defend and serve the people of the United States, we are students too, with our own independent beliefs, political views, and thoughts."[29]

Carol Cohen, an associate dean of Brown and the coordinator for ROTC, believes ROTC is "incompatible with the principles of a liberal arts education."[30] With friends like Dean Cohen, who needs enemies? Some members of Brown's faculty apparently agree. One Brown professor argues, "public and private universities shouldn't be in the business of making better officers . . . the missions of the military and a liberal arts education are fundamentally different."[31]

Princeton, Dartmouth, and the University of Pennsylvania have ROTC programs. One Princeton ROTC student we spoke with who told us he had had no negative experiences, however, recalled his instructor being heckled on campus as a "baby killer." (The instructor replied, "I defend your right to say that, and someday you may thank me.")

More typical is a more overtly benign but pernicious feeling that "it" is "not for people like us." Paradoxically, the same individuals who may be moved to decry the fact that the military recruits more among less-advantaged groups still do their best to prevent those who are more advantaged from learning about service through on-campus representation.

---

29. "ROTC Cadets Are Students, Not Robots," *Brown Daily Herald,* January 27, 2005.
30. Aidan Levy, "Interest in ROTC Minimal at Brown Despite Debate at Other Ivies," *Brown Daily Herald,* February 15, 2005.
31. Ibid. Catherine Lutz, professor of anthropology, quoted.

We are not the only people to note the elitism that has deformed the view of the military on many American campuses. After reading Frank and John's book *Keeping Faith,* former president George Herbert Walker Bush wrote to Frank:

September 24, 2002
Dear Frank,

... There's a lot about being President that I do *not* miss. But I *do* miss working with our great military. I respect those who serve. I realize that even today, even after 9/11, there are still those who look down on our men/women who serve. Why do several Ivy League schools still hate the military? There's a cultural arrogance ...
All the best,
George Bush

THE MEDIA

Books have been written about the tension between members of the mainstream media and the military, such as *The Media and the Military: Why the Press Cannot Be Trusted to Cover a War,* by William V. Kennedy. Kennedy charges that the media lacks the training and understanding of military issues to cover wars competently, and moreover that cultural biases lead editors to shy away from positive coverage. For instance, Kennedy recounts the words of journalist Fred Reeds, who reports, "I know that I can easily sell articles criticizing the military, but that a piece praising anything the services do is nearly impossible to peddle. In conversation, magazine editors almost without exception are hostile and contemptuous of the military."[32]

---

32. William V. Kennedy, *The Media and the Military: Why the Press Cannot Be Trusted to Cover a War* (New York: Praeger Publishers, 1993), p. 14.

Many in the media dispute these allegations. Moreover, we suspect that the media feels that problems are news, support isn't. In the interest of unbiased reporting, they believe that when they have a statement from a member of the military showing support for his or her service, they feel the need to go to great lengths to show that support as only half of the story. In one telling incident in late 2003, Frank received a call from a National Public Radio reporter soon after he did a commentary for their news program *All Things Considered.* She asked Frank if he could help her find a quote to balance what she called "all the pro-military stuff typical of military people" for a story she was producing on military families. She had been having trouble rounding up a negative "balancing quote."

"You're in touch with a lot of those people," she said. "You must know somebody who will share their bad experience with us."

In fact, Frank was able to help her out. He pointed her to a woman having trouble with the medical benefits due her wounded son—she had written to Frank blasting the Department of Veterans Affairs. Two days later the reporter called Frank again.

"You wouldn't have another source, would you?" she asked.

"How come?" asked Frank.

"Well, she said that in spite of her problems with the paperwork, she's proud of her son's service and won't make the sort of statement I'm looking for."

Of course, there are disgruntled members of the military family. However, quoting "both sides," say, from mothers whose sons have been killed in combat, may paint a false picture for the public, who are left assuming there is some sort of fifty-fifty split between those in the military who feel military service is a positive vocation and those who don't. And yet, Frank was hard-pressed to find that one disgruntled mother from a file of literally several thousand e-mails in response to his books and newspaper articles. He had plenty of people's letters complaining about some aspect of service or their fears for their children's safety, but the complaints were not about military service per se.

However, what the media do not report on is perhaps even more telling than what they do write. The newspapers read by the elite classes—the *New York Times,* the *Washington Post,* and the *Los Angeles Times*—seem infrequently to cover heroism among those who serve. Yet heroism strikes us as one of the most admirable and impressive qualities that military service inspires in those who volunteer. And without understanding heroism the public can't begin to understand why so many military men and women are inspired to reenlist. For newspapers trying to let readers know what military life is like—or about what motivates military people—to ignore individual stories about heroism is to leave the public uninformed.

Often very ordinary people do stunningly heroic things while in uniform. In previous eras, it was common for the newspapers just mentioned to cover these stories often, to give them prominent attention in a front section. Today most of the time our prestige press seems to regard the heroism of their fellow Americans in uniform as something not fit for publication. Perhaps they don't want to have anything in their pages mistaken for the kind of cheering section that the press provided when we were in the Second World War. During that war, the line between government propaganda and journalism was crossed often (most famously by a *New York Times* reporter who enthusiastically covered the dropping of the atomic bomb and later went so far as to disparage the truth of reports from Hiroshima and Nagasaki that the Japanese were dying of radiation poisoning.)

Our elite press may think that reporting acts of heroism plays into the hands of the Pentagon's propaganda spinners or may boost the stature of a disliked administration or policy. Perhaps they do not want the glory of any individual soldier to rub off on political leaders or a war they might oppose. Or perhaps they simply don't know about heroism, because they don't understand what the military does and they don't get close enough to see it. This may be another price we pay for the fact that very few editors and reporters—who are predominantly drawn from the ranks of the Ivy League—have anyone in their own family serving, as reporters and editors often did in World War II. We have a hunch that regardless of their politics, if the senior editors and reporters at our biggest newspapers had a child in uniform, they might approach reporting on the heroic acts of their child's fellow warriors, on whom their child's life depended, rather differently.

It is a shame that stories of heroism are ignored. A whole generation of Americans is growing up without knowing that very ordinary young people such as themselves can rise to great heights of bravery. What follows are some of the hundreds of recent stories that were not covered in the major media. (These stories were reported directly to us by family members, in the independent *The Marine Corps Times,* or in the "military interest" section of the local paper in Kathy's military base community.[33])

Battalion commander Lieutenant Colonel Matthew Lopez's convoy was ambushed in Iraq in April 2004. During the fighting, an AK-47 round slammed into Lopez's bulletproof vest and ricocheted off into his back. He fought back, and he brought the convoy to a safe place to evacuate five wounded Marines, plus an Iraqi translator. Lopez himself refused to be evacuated. He then led the entire battalion in a forty-eight-hour fight against hundreds of insurgents, while his wound continued bleeding through his bandages and cammies. His battalion eventually routed the insurgents.

Paul Smith was a combat engineer—which means he was trained to provide construction and demolition, often under fire in tough

---

33. Lisa Hoffman, "Roster of American Combat Heroes in Iraq Is Rich," Scripps Howard News Service, May 3, 2005.

terrain in Iraq. In 2003 he was with a group of sixteen traveling in an armored personnel carrier, trapped by one hundred Special Republican Guard fighters with rocket-propelled grenades, mortars, and assault rifles. The crew of the armored vehicle carrying the Americans were wounded and unable to drive. Smith raised himself out of the personnel carrier, took control of a mounted gun, and fired five hundred rounds while he was hit repeatedly, to the extent that the ceramic plate on his flak jacket was shattered. Smith saved the lives of every man in his squad, covering them while they made it to safety. In the end, fifty of the enemy were killed. Of the Americans, only Paul Smith died.

In 2004, Brad Kasal led a handful of Marines into an insurgent-held house to rescue three trapped and wounded comrades. During the course of the rescue, Kasal was shot seven times and used his body to shield an injured comrade, absorbing forty pieces of shrapnel. He survived, as did the injured Marine and all but one of the other Marines.

Twenty-three-year-old Todd Bolding was handing out soccer balls and school supplies to a group of Iraqi children, when the children came under attack by a rocket-propelled grenade. Bolding did not retreat to safety, but rushed to the children, struggling to treat their wounds, when the attackers struck again. Bolding was fatally wounded in the continuing attack.

Jason Hendrix spent his own savings to buy other soldiers night-vision goggles, flashlights, and face masks. He donated his rations regularly to hungry Iraqi children, and gave his Christmas leave to a friend to go home and see his new baby. In February 2004, Jason's squad deliberately attracted fire in an attempt to draw enemy fire away from advancing troops. When the vehicles in his squad burst into flames, Jason ran back to the various vehicles repeatedly in an attempt to save his comrades. He managed to save six soldiers from fiery deaths before an explosion killed him.

We do get body counts on page one: "Iraq Deaths Top 2,000" or "14 Soldiers Die in One Attack." And in some papers the names of the dead are listed in small boxes tucked away deep in the paper—name, and rank, and day of death. The body counts seem to be disconnected from any moral meaning of individual sacrifice. What was accomplished during the mission? What is the meaning behind the number? Who were the heroes in the engagement? What did they do? Who struggled to save them as brave medics shielded fallen comrades with their bodies, as an Army nurse sat up for seventy hours holding one soldier's hand? As a daring pilot flew a bad-weather air-to-air refueling mission so a wounded soldier being airlifted to treatment might have a chance to survive? Who speaks for America's heroes?

⋆

Through his e-mail correspondence Frank became friends with Mindy Evnin, the mother of Mark Evnin, a young Marine killed in Iraq during the early stages of that war. Mindy is a psychotherapist and not what people might picture as a typical military parent. Mark was her only child. In September of 2005, several years after Mark was killed, Frank asked Mindy for the details surrounding her son's death. In answer Mindy wrote:

> This [answering Frank's question] has been much harder to do than I realized. I went back to look at some of the material that I had about Mark and his death, and saw that the story is always slightly different in each account. I know it doesn't matter, but I got stuck on that for a while, and then spent a couple of hours rereading articles and letters that I hadn't looked at in a long time. It made me sadder than I realized it would. . . .

Mark was a Scout Sniper (of which he was very proud), assigned to the 3/4 [Third Battalion, Fourth Marine Regiment] based in Twenty Nine Palms, CA. . . . Mark served as the spotter for the sniper team and was also the Humvee driver. The 3/4 crossed into Iraq on March 20, 2003. On April 3, they were sent to the city of Al Kut, where there were reported to be enemy fedayeen. The job of the 3/4 was to suppress any resistance in the city. The convoy came to a stretch in the road with a palm grove on the right and a sandy patch on the left. After the tanks had passed, the battalion was ambushed with machine guns and RPGs [rocket-propelled grenades] from the palm grove.

An amtrac [amphibious vehicle] pulled to the side of the road at a 45-degree angle, and Mark parked the Humvee behind the amtrac. The area was filled with smoke from all the gunfire. The Sgt. Major told Mark to get his M203 (hybrid M16 and single-shot grenade launcher) and led him to the rear of the amtrac. He told Mark to "take out" the RPK (no idea what that is) firing out of a bunker at the far end of the grove. Mark loaded the weapon, stepped out from behind the amtrac, and fired at the target. He then stepped back behind the amtrac to reload. I'm not sure how many grenades he launched that way. After reloading when he stepped out from behind the amtrac to fire again, an Iraqi in the grove sprayed a burst of machine-gun fire and hit Mark below his Kevlar vest. At first he wasn't sure what happened, and then fell to the ground. The Sgt. Major, who was about 15 yards away behind a mound of dirt, ran over and dragged him behind the mound of dirt. Mark was "bitching about how he couldn't believe he had been hit." The Sgt. Major and the medic loosened his clothes and saw two holes in his abdomen (not much blood). Mark was in pain but coherent.

While waiting for a Humvee to evacuate Mark to the aid station, the Sgt. Major said, "Look on the bright side, Evnin, you won't have to put up with me anymore." Mark's response was, "Sgt. Major, you're the biggest asshole I've ever worked for." I think he said it to break the tension, and to make the Sgt. Major feel better. He also probably said it because he could get away with it, and it would be a great story to tell the guys later . . .

Mark was evacuated to the aid station, where Chaplain Grove of the 3/4 saw Mark and read the Jewish prayers over him. As he finished the first prayer, Mark said, "Good to go, Chaplain." I think that Mark could sense the chaplain's nervousness and unfamiliarity with the Jewish prayer, and he wanted to reassure him that all was okay. As the Chaplain began reading the 23rd Psalm, Mark interrupted to reassure him (and probably himself), and said, "I'm not going to die." I think that to the last he didn't want to worry anyone. He always had a very kind soul.

Frank, I don't know if Mark was a "hero." He did what he was asked to do, and he did it without hesitation, as did many Marines, knowing that the firefight was dangerous. Maybe that is heroic. It certainly was bravery, and honor and duty. Part of the citation for his medal says, that, "Corporal Evnin's initiative, perseverance, and total dedication to duty reflected great credit upon himself and were in keeping with the highest traditions of the Marine Corps and the United States Naval Service."

Frank, one more thing—the Sgt. Major told me that during the war, one of his jobs was to drive around to see where the action was, and do some reconnaissance. He would have Mark pull over to the side of the road, and tell him to stay with the Humvee, in part to protect it. . . . Frequently he would turn around to find Mark following him. When he asked Mark what the hell he was doing, Mark would explain that he thought it was important to watch the Sgt. Major's back, more than watching the Humvee. I think that was brave. Mark was doing something potentially dangerous that was not asked of him.

Okay, I'm done. No more e-mails tonight. I'm going to my book club and going to try to relax.
Mindy

When the officer came to her door with the news that Mark was dead, Mindy, seeing the desperate sadness stamped on the young Marine's face, reached out to him. Before he could break the news she said, "This must be so terribly hard for you to do. Thank you."

Has the media done all it can to introduce the American public to people like Mark and Mindy Evnin? It seems to us that we need to know more about women like Mindy who comforted a frightened young Marine in her own moment of supreme anguish. We need to know that her dying son tried to help a nervous chaplain as he read a prayer over him. We need to know these things, not because they glorify war—they don't—or boost the standing of political leaders, but because Mindy's and Mark's lives give us a glimpse of grace.

We think that Mindy Evnin has written the best description of what service is: "I don't know if Mark was a 'hero.' He did what he was asked to do, and he did it without hesitation . . . knowing that the firefight was dangerous. Maybe that is heroic. It certainly was bravery, and honor and duty."

There are a number of journalists who write about the military with substance and understanding—columnists William Safire, George Will, and Thomas Friedman leap to mind; and of course *Washington*

Post writer Thomas Ricks, not to mention Michael M. Phillips of the *Wall Street Journal.* And *Rolling Stone* magazine writers have written thoughtful and compelling stories about West Point and the Iraq War.[34]

Ricks wrote a well-received book about the Marine Corps, spending enough time with a platoon going through boot camp that he is practically an honorary Marine. Two of Ricks's journalism mentors were former Marines. In fact, many of the journalists who seem to "get" the military—such as David Lipsky, the author of *Absolutely American,* about four years at West Point, and Evan Wright, author of *Generation Kill,* about a platoon of recon Marines in Iraq— are the ones who've spent the most personal time with our men and women. But how many of today's journalists, lacking mentors like Ricks's or personal experience like Lipsky's and Wright's or actual time in uniform, will bring that insight to their coverage of world affairs?

Wall Street Journal staff reporter Michael M. Phillips was embedded with the Third Battalion, Seventh Marines in Iraq and did four tours with them. As a result of this very personal connection he was deeply moved when he heard that Jason Dunham, a twenty-two-year-old corporal from the one-stoplight town of Scio, New York, died after shielding his comrades from a grenade.

When Michael Philips wrote Jason Dunham's story, and the stories of all the incredibly selfless military personnel, medics, soldiers, and nurses, who tried to save Jason Dunham's life, the *Journal* did indeed give it page-one treatment. When Frank asked Michael Phillips about the reaction to the story, he told Frank that his paper got over three hundred e-mails and letters.

Evidently there is a hunger for inspiring information about those

---

34. David Lipsky, *Absolutely American: Four Years at West Point* (New York: Houghton Mifflin, 2003); Evan Wright, *Generation Kill* (New York: Putnam, 2004).

we pay lip service to as "our best young men and women" but rarely get to know. The public reaction was so strong that Broadway Books contacted Michael Phillips and asked him to turn the story into a book, *The Gift of Valor.*

The Gift of Valor is a piece of extraordinary wartime writing. It is not about politics but about character, the character of a young American of whom we can all be proud. It is a study in existential courage that that gives new meaning to the word *sacrifice.*

Journalists such as Michael Phillips and the others we have just mentioned are the exceptions. The more usual discomfort with discussing heroism also shows in discussions about military recruiting. The papers all eagerly cover shortfalls. But they didn't seem to be able to explain why even in the midst of the Iraq War's growing unpopularity in 2005, and in spite of the Army shortfalls in recruiting of new soldiers, the reenlistment numbers for all the services went up.

Words like *honor, valor, heroism, selflessness, loyalty,* don't easily find their way onto the pages of our leading newspapers, at least not unless they are bracketed by quotation marks. But, "re-upping" bonuses aside, the values implicit in those rarely used words seem to us to be the only good explanation of why so many of our war-weary troops renewed their military commitment and wouldn't leave their brothers and sisters to fight on alone, even in an unpopular war. Again, where are the many stories of the soldiers who canceled long-term plans to start college or return to civilian life so they could reenlist for altruistic reasons?

In mid-2005 the *New York Times* editorialized about the Army's recruiting problems, "The Army's inability to recruit enough soldiers to sustain its worldwide commitments is already serious, becoming alarming, and poses a real threat to the future of America's all-volunteer military. That should be ringing bells in the Congress and the country and creating intense political pressure to address the underlying problems. They range from intolerable strains on morale and readiness as a result of having too few troops in Iraq to absurd and offensive policies that limit the Army's ability to make full use of its female soldiers and openly gay men and women wanting to serve their country."

The *Times* concludes the editorial, "Instead of managing its recruitment numbers and playing dangerous games with quality standards, the Army needs to level with the public and Congress about what it will take to meet the nation's defense needs and restore the health of the volunteer force that has served America well."

Here's what the *Times* might logically have been expected to conclude: "The all-volunteer force is not serving our country well. It is allowing the most privileged Americans to do in our country what Europeans have been accused by Americans of doing for the last fifty years: hiding behind the American military while profiting from it, yet contributing little to our common defense. Instead of managing its recruitment numbers and playing dangerous games with quality standards, the Army needs to call upon America's upper middle classes and upper classes to begin shouldering their responsibility and to volunteer proportionate to their numbers. In that spirit, the *New York Times* has invited recruiters to meet with those of us at the paper who are physically and age-qualified to serve."

Seems laughably impossible, doesn't it? Why? Perhaps for the same reason that it might have seemed impossible in 1800 for there to be a Jewish president of Harvard or in 1959 for there to be a black editor at the *New York Times*. Assumptions about class, race, gender, and other social constructs aren't examined until they are questioned, and people who think they are the most enlightened often seem to have the biggest unaddressed prejudicial assumptions.

To some enterprising writer out there, may we suggest a Pulitzer-caliber series of in-depth pieces comparing the family histories of military service and nonservice in the Bush dynasty, the Sulzberger family (owners of the *New York Times*), and the Kennedy clan. It is instructive to see that all the Kennedy brothers served but none of the Kennedy cousins did, and that Arthur Ochs Sulzberger, chairman of the *Times,* served but none of his children or grandchildren did, and that Bush senior served with great distinction but none of the Bush grandchildren have volunteered.

Here's the closing paragraph: "The collective answer of our elites, of the right, left, and center, to John F. Kennedy's challenge 'Ask not what your country can do for you; ask what you can do for your country,' seems to be, 'Not much!' when it comes to the post-Vietnam privileged classes' willingness to serve our country in our military."

THE MOVIES

What sort of movies have fueled and reinforced the privileged classes' view of the military over the last several decades since Vietnam? There have been many recent films and TV series, such as *Saving Private Ryan* and *Band of Brothers,* that have painted an inspiring portrait of military service. But for many Americans who have no direct exposure to the military, other important movies have served as justification for negative feelings about this institution. Here is a short list of ones that strike us as particularly significant:

> *American Beauty*
> *Apocalypse Now*
> *Born on the Fourth of July*
> *The Deer Hunter*
> *Fahrenheit 9/11*
> *Full Metal Jacket*

The Great Santini
Platoon
The Thin Red Line

In *Full Metal Jacket* a sadistic drill instructor drives one recruit to suicide and prepares the rest to become hardened killers in what is portrayed as a bankrupt war. In *Born on the Fourth of July* the "good" soldiers are dissidents. In *Platoon* the men who serve are either sensitive victims or butchers. In *Apocalypse Now* military men are again victims or deranged killers serving an evil system. *The Deer Hunter* portrays the communists in Vietnam as evil (the movie was therefore picketed at the Oscars by Jane Fonda) but also shows American soldiers and their families being wrecked by their association with the military, which is exemplified in one soldier's playing Russian roulette till he kills himself. In *The Thin Red Line* the military is shown squandering the lives of soldiers (victims again). The hero is an officer who will not send his men into battle against the Japanese. In *American Beauty* the villain is a repressed gay psychopathic former Marine colonel. His military memorabilia mingles with Nazi artifacts. (Nothing too subtle!) In *The Great Santini* Robert Duvall gives a stunningly memorable performance as a Marine pilot. He is the quintessential hard-ass, action-craving Marine. His love of the Corps and his addiction to action makes him a bad father, out of touch with his family. In the last analysis, the film reinforces a certain cliché: the military is full of people driven by some sort of inner demon to live too fast, too hard, people out of touch with the kinder, gentler side of life.

The movies listed above make some valid points about the banality of service and about war, suffering, and patriotism that verges on jingoism. They portray situations that do arise in war. Sometimes wounded prisoners do get shot. Sometimes atrocities occur. Some warriors are hard cases. Some generals don't give a damn about their men and women. And many men and women who have served and fought find some truth in several or all of these movies.

But taken together these films and many, many more besides, have reinforced a generation's highly politicized and jaded view of the military as a place where only victims and/or sadists serve the illegitimate ends of one or another despised administration. Above all, the fundamental need for military service is never acknowledged.

Michael Moore's *Fahrenheit 9/11* serves as an example of the aggregate attitudes displayed in all the films we mention above. Moore "sympathizes" with our military men and women as exploited victims taken for a ride by callous or stupid recruiters manipulating recruits' poverty or lack of education. Why would anyone join who had a scholarship to college, medical benefits, or a good union job?

Moore edits in out-of-context footage of jumpy teenagers in uniform talking about the music they listen to when they are getting shot at and shooting back. Macho swaggering semiliterate statements from a few immature soldiers are taken out of context, a context where they were trying to pump themselves up to face battle. Moore's message: the military is a crude, violent place full of teenage Neanderthals, war is always wrong and the only good people in the military were tricked into joining, the rest are insensitive killers.

THE MILITARY—SURROGATE FOR THE CULTURE WARS

For the opinion makers and most of our political leadership on the left or right, service is no longer thought of as the common duty of all citizens. More often than not when the elites take notice, the military is used as a surrogate to fight larger political and culture-war battles.

The so-called swift boat veterans did nothing to enhance the reputation of the military as an institution above politics by using footage of Vietnam in their anti–John Kerry commercials, and by trying to rope other veterans into their transparent political crusade. And President Bush and his slick media machine did not honor the military when they used men in uniform as a good backdrop for glib photo ops.

The military is not a political creature of the right or left. (On which, more later.) It is made up of real human beings; good, bad, and all points in between, just like the rest of the country. And the military has always been all-too human, as the many atrocities our side committed even in the "good war"—World War II—prove. But all that does not answer these questions: Do we need a military? If we do, who should serve? If our men and women in uniform are not seen as all of our sons and daughters, then whose are they? Have we lost a sense of community, and perhaps of citizenship as well?

3. The Military's View of What It Does

★★★★★★★★★★★★★★★★★★★★

The idea that the military does not encourage critical thinking is pure b.s. I learned more in my seven years as an enlisted man in the Marines, than in all my years in college and grad school combined.

—John Raughter, editor,
The American Legion Magazine

Frank and Kathy

Military people do not argue that military life is a utopia. It is a bureaucracy, with many of the attendant faults, and it is a structure where individuals have power over each other, with sufficient incidents of people abusing that power to fill books. But every survey and study shows that today's volunteers see a great deal of good in what they do.

The fact is that most military people experience their service as enriching—in ways that have nothing to do with perks, money, or technical skills. This is as true for the few most privileged who serve as it is for the solidly working-class majority. As members of the military family, the two of us feel the same.

Certainly we have both experienced lonely frightening nights and days while our loved ones were in danger—Kathy's husband, Greg, was in combat as we wrote. And we are all for making the services better. But the salutary side of our experiences—the sense of having shared in a son's and husband's sacrifice as our contribution to our national security, the sense of accomplishment that comes from supporting our loved one's service, of keeping the home fires burning—has been overwhelmingly positive. And we are typical of other military families in that sense of accomplishment.

Frank

After I began to write a series of opinion pieces about the experience of being a military parent, I received and answered over four thousand e-mails in the course of five years. Not only were the letters interesting and often moving, but the very size of the response told me I had hit a nerve that was out of all proportion to what an author—at least in my experience—can normally expect his or her work to generate. Military people told me I was expressing something that a lot of them thought did not get said enough—that military service is uplifting to the people who take that path in ways most opinion makers do not seem to understand.

The letters I got show military pride, but many also demonstrate the sense of frustration that so many of us in the military family feel about being marginalized. Here are some excerpts. They tell their own story:

> I had the good fortune to grow up in an affluent Washington suburb, go to a "nuclear-free" liberal arts college, and enjoy a variety of career options. I chose to become a Marine officer, serving as a pilot in places most Americans would be hard-pressed

to find on a map: the Philippines, Somalia, Djibouti. I came to my decision because my parents and other role models instilled in me the concept of public service—of becoming part of something greater than myself. As a result, I have had the honor to work with incredibly dedicated young men and women from all walks of life who are considered blue-collar cannon fodder in many elitist circles. It is my hope, in our post-9/11 introspection, that America will encourage more young people to give back to our society, whether with a two-year stint in the Peace Corps or as a member of the armed forces.

Matt Green

Military service isn't about intimidating our neighbors, or militarizing our youth or citizenry. It is about homogenizing our society. It is about getting people out of their ghettos, both physical and intellectual. It is about overcoming racial and cultural differences and divisiveness to achieve a common goal. It teaches pride in self for succeeding in a difficult course, and pride in our country and society. It teaches responsibility for self and others that depend on you in a way that cannot be taught elsewhere.

David H. Sparkman

My son graduated from school a semester early with a 4.0 GPA and score of 24 on the ACT, and joined the Marines six months before 9/11. I actually admired the decision. I couldn't fault a young man who was decisive about his future and goals. I'd raised him to find himself and follow his dreams. He did. But no one on either side of the family had ever been in the military. My own sensibilities are decidedly not "Gung-Ho."

At boot camp graduation I noticed the framed Medal of Honor affidavits. Too easily, I envisioned my son in the same situation on those plaques, employing the same courageous and fatal tactics. I was proud to know he had that courage already, and terrified that he might one day have the opportunity to use it. I knew that with his character and the training he'd just completed, he would not hesitate. I remembered reading a study some years back that gave evidence that American men in combat more readily defended the lives of their friends than they did their own. It's hard not to admire, even revere, these young men.

Wayne Sheldrake

I don't know any ex-serviceman who doesn't agree with Yoda when he said, "Do or do not. There is no try." Your son John will have the far better education when his five years are up than any of his high school peers. There is no college anywhere that could give him the responsibility, earned (not donated) self-esteem, and the real-life experience (whether of commercial value or not) that his signal intelligence job brings him.

Rick Rogovy

I saw your interview on CSPAN last week. I share your concerns regarding the empty rhetoric from the administration and the general disdain of my fellow academics. Many in the academy seem to show personal concern for those serving. With the end of the draft and the return to a professional military, it is vital that we do not develop an isolated officer class with few links to our larger society. The progressively conservative drift of the professional military is not healthy for the democratic process. It is therefore incumbent on academics and elites to better understand the military and on members of the military to stay open to ideas from the larger society.

Unlike myself—I enlisted at seventeen and didn't really understand the consequences—my son was a graduate from an elite university and was not faced with a draft. Although he has almost fifteen years in the Army, he remains open-minded and connected to intellectual life. Through our regular correspondence and my observation of the positions of numerous retired officers, I am beginning to detect some awareness on the part of thinking members of the military that their assumptions about support may be somewhat faulty.

During and after Vietnam, most members of the military came to accept as a given that all liberals despised them and all conservatives supported them. The reality, of course, is far more complex. As they come to see that much of the "support" is hollow and does not include a willingness to sacrifice or serve, liberals could do much to rebalance the perspective of the military. A few tentative steps have been made. . . . You might find the following letter, written from [my son, while serving in] Iraq, heartening. I did . . . [see next letter].
William J. Vizzard

People are often surprised by my liberal leanings and ask how I can serve in the military and be a Democrat (as if those are somehow fundamentally incompatible). When I feel like answering, I tell them that I serve because I believe in the promise of the United States regardless of the practice on any given day. I believe that with all its many flaws and despite the periodic efforts of the American people to self-destruct, our system of government and our society are the most self-correcting in the world. I believe that we have achieved steady progress (yes, the dreaded P word, all you relativist academics) from a slaveholding oligarchy with less than 10 percent suffrage, to a wage-slaving oligarchy with the government a wholly owned subsidiary of the Standard Oil Company and U.S. Steel, to a society in which Rosa Parks can ride in the front of the bus and Colin Powell can be secretary of state and Dick Cheney can defend (sort of) gay marriage. If the fight were easy, it wouldn't have to be fought.

I am sitting in one of the most hellish places on earth, surrounded by five million people who hate me and several thousand who try to kill me regularly, but I am also surrounded by a couple of thousand young men and women who are putting their lives on the line for things in which they believe. They may have been misled, but that does not diminish their courage and commitment. A cynic might say that they joined for college money or because they had few other options, and that these are selfish reasons, but they are not selfish. Those are attempts to better themselves, and thereby better their communities. With all their many flaws, and despite the fact that they are mostly Republicans, they give me hope.

This is not a great day for our country, but there have been worse days. I believe that most of us will survive another four years, but I am unutterably sad about the thousand or two or five here around me who will not.
James Vizzard

I am the first American born of my family, which migrated here in 1968. We were financially challenged but that's all. All my life I had been told by my family we came here for a better way of life for us, their children. I distinctly remember when I was seventeen; my uncle said to me, "You'll have every opportunity to become anything you want. You are an American Citizen!

Two months prior to graduating high school, I enlisted in the U.S. Navy's Delayed Entry Program, rather than going to college as my family expected. I felt at the time it was my responsibility to pay back what our country provided for us all.

I know my family and friends could never understand why I joined or ever realize how dangerous the carrier flight deck could be. Every cruise we deployed on, whether peace or war time, we always lost a few souls. It's just the nature of the beast. I left the military, and hold degrees in engineering and business. But when people visit my home, the place they gaze upon each time is my shadow box of medals, and I remember, and feel the pride I felt when I first enlisted. The critics of the military will never know what we in the military family share.
Michael Marguliz

Permit me to add my own testimonial to those quoted above. I've discovered that the person who volunteers is changed by military service, and that those who love him change too. In my case, I've found it is hard to be as selfish when my son has put his life on the line for his family, neighbors, and country. A small, very trivial illustration: before John enlisted I rarely bothered to go to our local town meetings. But as I began to think about John's service, it seemed the least I could do was participate in the democracy he was defending.

Before, I would never have pictured myself stamping envelopes at a neighbor's kitchen table to help in a mailing for a local selectman candidate or standing on a street corner holding a sign on election day. Like most of the better-off folks in my area, I used my home as a bedroom and office and let the "locals" take care of the nondescript jobs such as town selectmen. We were too busy doing "important" things to do anything as mundane as help run our small town.

After John got back from his first deployment, Genie asked him, "Is your childhood over?"

"Yup, it's gone," John answered.

As he said this I thought that he wasn't the only person in our family to have grown up. To some extent, I had too. And this is part of the value of an individual's service. It not only imbues the soldier, Marine, airman, sailor, or Coast Guardsman with values and a deep sense of connection to the country—but it accomplishes that same alchemy with the whole network of people surrounding them, with their parents, spouses, children, and friends.

With John's service I was suddenly aware that my real guardian angels were men and women with whom I had little in common, except that we shared a single heart: someone we loved was in uniform and they were awake as we slept, cold when we were warm, hungry when we were filled, tired when we were rested, in danger when we were safe. And my small town no longer seemed like just a place to park my body while I focused on my Boston and New York contacts. My town seemed rather more like a hometown that had given many sons just like mine. It was a place with a little war memorial that might someday have my son's name on it if he didn't come home. What had I done to be so high-and-mighty and proud of anyway? What had I ever done for anyone? And "these people" had been sending their sons and daughters to serve long before I lost a moment's sleep over the well-being of mine.

My illusion of independence was gone. The words *"We're all in this together"* took on a new meaning.

My son came home alive because other Marines, soldiers, airmen, sailors, and Coast Guardsmen made his return possible. He came home healthy because the sons and daughters of strangers risked their lives for him. He came home because men and women I'll never meet who fought in other wars laid down a tradition of discipline and excellence that John's drill instructors maintained when they trained my boy. He came home because our men and women all along the way and all over the globe did their jobs. I owed them. I owed their families. I always will.

The highest compliment that I knew how to give John when he completed his time of service was, "Your drill instructors would be proud of the job you did." And the only thing that John said was bothering him was that so many of the people he knew outside the military kept saying things to him along the lines of *what a relief it must be to be out.*

"That really pisses me off," John told me. "I tell them, it's not a 'relief.' I was sad to leave, but I wanted to go to college. I enjoyed being in the Marines but have some things I need to do now. I am not 'glad' to be out; I've just moved on to something else, that's all. I could have stayed in and been happy. It was a tough call."

Kathy

I was living a fairly glamorous life in 1995, when I was thirty. I had left the White House for Manhattan, and was working for billionaire Ronald Perelman and his wife. My job involved helping the couple to give their money away, through their foundations and political interests. It was a great job, a great work atmosphere. My office furniture included lovely antiques; the office had works by Modigliani, Giacometti, Frank Stella, Picasso. And the terms were generous. Perks included use of the corporate box at Knicks' games and tickets to the U.S. Open. As one young woman who knew my story said to me years later, when I was married and living on a Marine base, "You gave that up for *this?*"

Back then, I belonged to the demiworld of strivers who support hyperwealthy people. We served the megarich as stockbrokers or $500,000-a-year gofers with job titles like "executive vice president." Our goal was money, access, status. The means seemed to include stretching the truth. Most people I ran across exaggerated accomplishments; padded résumés, which were rolled out at the slightest provocation; took credit where it may not have been due. From watching some of the extraordinary public instances of lying at that time—Larry Lawrence, for example, who had spun a tale of heroism in World War II that was completely false, and whose widow, Shelia, had to have him disinterred from Arlington Cemetery—I knew that cognitive dissonance acts in such a way that people cannot comfortably both lie and know they are lying. The only way to resolve the internal tension of believing and saying two different things is to come to believe your own lies.

The Marines I have gotten to know have thrown that world into sharp relief. They are not impressed or unimpressed by the names of anyone I met back then. Marines don't try to tell anyone about their big accomplishments. The Marines who are my neighbors have a wonderful self-confidence that puts them at ease wherever they are, and it stands in contrast to the posturing I saw. A family member of mine said some of the Marines I introduced them to seemed like men and women out of another era.

What does this have to do with how those of us in the military family think of ourselves? It goes back to the idea that the things you do shape the person you become. Having learned the Marine Corps culture, I see that much of what I find so attractive and admirable about the Marines I meet daily on base, their character and self-confidence, is cultivated by the military. And perhaps a few of the people I crossed paths with in New York and Washington might have benefited from a dose of whatever it is that makes Marines who they are—even a tour of duty in the military before heading out to rule the universe.

Kathy and Frank

We decided to reach out to some young people in uniform who are "winners" according to the American definition of academic success. They got those Ivy League degrees that are so coveted. And these days they are a tiny minority in our military. We surveyed alumni, primarily at Princeton, but from other top schools such as Amherst and Harvard Law School, who bucked the trend and recently chose to go into military service. We asked them about their experiences. Here are some of their responses:

> Whenever I tell someone that I'll be graduating from Princeton and going into the Marine Corps, a typical response is "Oh, why are you doing that?" Most of my friends will be going into the financial world or law school. I think it is the same competitive drive that took us to Princeton then Wall Street or a top law school that steered me to the Marine Corps.
>
> When my friends wake up each morning, will they be able to say that their colleagues are motivated by more than a personal desire to succeed? I doubt it. I have earned the honor and the privilege of one day leading Marines; that's an awesome responsibility unlike any other on earth. When that day comes, I want to be able to say that I have worked as hard as I can and that I have learned as much as I can, so that those junior Marines I am responsible for can say that the Marine Corps has provided them their due. This responsibility imbues every day of training with a deep sense of purpose. Becoming a Marine officer goes way beyond duty to your country or continuing family traditions. A second lieutenant infantry officer has in his hands the life and well-being of forty young men, some older than himself. Becoming an officer in the United States Marine Corps is not a job, it is a calling.
> Eric Chase (Princeton 2006)

> Thus far, I have loved my time in the military. The military has provided me both incredible challenges and personal satisfaction. At the age of twenty-three, I was given the responsibility of solo-piloting a $30-million warplane. The challenge

of USAF pilot training (and other combat-related military functions) is one not easily replicated in the civilian world. It builds confidence and leadership ability. Personally, I also get much satisfaction knowing my efforts have improved the security of our nation in a small but tangible manner. I would most definitely do it again.

Raj Shah (Princeton 2000)

The military has given me some great learning experiences, some excellent opportunities for personal growth and leadership training, grounded my patriotism in reality, and also, has exposed me to people I wouldn't have met otherwise. That last thing is not inconsequential. The Army is still a more diverse place than most workplaces that Ivy Leaguers are in. In just my little Security and Intelligence section in Iraq, we had an African-American Muslim, a white Quaker, a white Jew, four white Catholics (one not-practicing), and a white Protestant female. I had the honor of reenlisting the Muslim guy while we were over there. The Army mixes "blue state" people and "red state" people and expects them to function.

Sometimes this works and sometimes it doesn't, but the Army isn't monolithic in the way that some areas of the country seem to be. My sister lives in San Francisco, and I doubt if she knows three people who will admit to being Republicans, and probably not a single honest-to-God conservative. Many people only know and work with others who think and believe the same things that they do. Part of this is of course about class, which is an uncomfortable subject for Americans, since we don't think we have classes per se.

As for why I've stayed in now that my obligation is over, I sometimes wonder that myself. I particularly wonder why now that I've been to Iraq. I've "seen the elephant" now, as the Civil War phrase went. I've paid back my obligation, been deployed twice, left in the middle of graduate school to be mobilized for the war in Iraq, served with honor, and was lucky enough to come home safely. That ought to be enough, surely. But I will probably stay in, at least until I have a family of my own. In part because of patriotism, in part because I've taken on board the values of the military enough that the Army as an organization is important to me, in part because I like the extra money, in part because I (often) like the work I do and the people I do it with, and in part because it's become a key element of my identity.

Philip F. Romanelli (Princeton 1992)

My military experience has probably given me more discipline and confidence that adversity can be mastered. As for why I stayed—protecting civil and human rights around the world for those in need has been part of my family's ethic in light of my father's own experiences as a Jewish refugee.

Peter Teil (Princeton 1985)

The military experience absolutely has benefited me. There is no doubt that I am an infinitely more mature person than I was when I graduated Princeton, and am so much more aware of the things I had taken for granted my entire life, such as how lucky I am to have the family I have, the opportunities I have had for things like a Princeton education, not to mention life's simple pleasures like a hot shower, a good meal, an evening at a baseball game, etc. After something like Ranger School, lots of other challenges that may have seemed daunting in the past seem pretty easy by comparison. I kind of felt this was my generation's time to "step up" to a challenge in the same way my grandfathers did in World War II. I will likely return to

school when my commitment is over, as my original intention was to serve, not necessarily to make it a career.
Will Bardenwerper (Princeton 1998)

I believe that a large part of my personality and leadership style extend from what I learned in the military. As a woman, I learned to stand up for myself and to expect to be treated equally with men. I learned that I can do more than I think I can. I also learned a lot about leadership and people.
Jeanne Dorweiler (Princeton 1993)

The experience one gains in the American military is invaluable. I think the primary benefit to me has been a better understanding of people. I have led and been led by many different Americans, most of whom I never would have met growing up in Connecticut or at Princeton University. My Princeton classmates who are professors at Harvard and vice presidents of Microsoft will never understand America and its citizens in the same way that I do. I credit the military with making me who I am today.

I admit that when I signed my scholarship contract, I thought I would most likely serve my commitment in the Army Reserve, and not have a full career on active duty. When I was commissioned, I thought I would serve my four years in the Army and then get out. I stayed in after my initial commitment because I wanted the opportunity to command an artillery battery. I am proud of what I do, and of how the Army has shaped me as a person.
Bob Bradford (Princeton 1988)

I graduated Amherst in 1998. Even though I didn't have to go into the Army, I felt that that didn't mean I shouldn't go. I felt like the country gave me a lot, and I wanted to give something

back. Plus I wanted to do something hard. I deferred JP Morgan for a year to do service; then I spent two years on Wall Street before being activated on 9/11 to participate in the rescue effort. I went to Baghdad for eleven months in '03 and '04. My worst day in Baghdad was better than my best day on Wall Street.
Paul Reickhoff (Princeton 1998)

The kinds of experiences expressed by our Ivy League interviewees are echoed by people we speak to from all walks of life. Military service brings people outside of themselves in ways they often don't expect, and often for the good. We thought this letter home from a corporal gives a good illustration of how that can happen:

February 19, 2004 Iraq
Dear Mom and Dad,
We were stopped in the desert outside of Fallujah. We had three detainees under our control that were captured in the act of attacking our Marines. Because we were in the open without any facilities around, the detainees were temporarily being held under the stars.
Around 3:00 AM, the wind started blowing hard and a sandstorm hit. The sky opened and the flying sand was joined by a downpour of rain. In the back of a truck, four Marines were trying to stay dry and get some sleep. The lieutenant who was in charge of providing security for the detainees approached this truck and opened up the back hatch. He ordered the Marines out. The Marines asked why, and he explained to them that he had to put the detainees in the back of the truck to protect them from the rain and sandstorm.
Word of this spread quickly and everyone was livid. We couldn't believe that our Marines were being kicked into the sandstorm/rainstorm so these detainees could stay dry. The next

day I was still angry and everyone was still talking about what had happened that night. Later in the day, after having time to cool down and think about the situation, I switched from being angry to being proud.

I love you and miss you lots.

Your son, Josh

Cpl. Joshua A. Mandel USMC

The richness of experience described above holds true for those who serve a single tour of duty and prepare for, but do not experience, combat. This is important, because actual combat is still the minority experience in the military. The vast majority of people in the U.S. military will never personally experience hostilities.

Louis Caldera, president of the University of New Mexico and former secretary of the army, who served from 1979 to 1983, mostly in Fort Dix, New Jersey, recounted his noncombatant experience this way:

I volunteered to serve, driven by the immigrant spirit to give something back to the country that had given so much to my family and me. Bookish, shy, a sheltered son; the military, with its emphasis on leadership development, moral and physical courage, and command presence and voice opened my eyes to the vast possibilities of life. Our mission in the Army—to be prepared to defend the nation and to serve wherever called in support of our nation's interest in the world—gave me a deeper appreciation for the forces, events, and people that shape the world we live in.[1]

Poll data and academic studies also support the argument that people who serve in the military have a high regard for military

---

1. Caldera, "The American Military and the Idea of Service," p. 149.

culture. An independent newspaper publisher called Military City, owned by Gannett, conducts an annual poll of active-duty officers and enlisted members from all services.[2] Each year, participants report very high satisfaction with their careers. In the most recently published survey, 85 percent surveyed were satisfied with their jobs. Eighty-two percent, would recommend a military career to others. Virtually all, or 91 percent, feel well-trained for their military job. Seventy-eight percent think that racial and ethnic minorities are treated more fairly in the military than in larger society.

According to the influential Triangle Institute for Security Studies (TISS) survey, military leaders see the military as promoting a culture that is above all, disciplined, loyal, hardworking, and honest. The percentage that identify these characteristics hovers around 95 percent on all issues. People in the military are much more likely than their civilian counterparts to see military culture as generous and creative.[3]

One of America's prominent think tanks, the Center for Strategic and International Studies (CSIS) in Washington, D.C., published a report titled "American Military Culture in the Twenty-first Century." The study found this culture to be "rich in the traditions of self-sacrifice, discipline, courage, physical rigor, and loyalty to comrades and country."[4]

---

2. Poll conducted by *Military City*, a publication of Gannett, which produces the *Navy Times, Army Times, Marine Times,* and *Air Force Times.* The 2005 poll was reported in January 2006. It may be viewed in its entirety on the Web site www.MilitaryCity.com. (Hereafter cited as *Military City* poll.)

3. Fewer than half of the military leaders would call the military culture creative—43.5 percent—but that figure is significantly smaller among civilian leaders without military experience—15.6 percent. Slightly over half of the military sample saw the culture as generous, compared with about a quarter of the civilian cohort. See table 1.16 1998 1999 TISS Survey, in *Soldiers and Civilians,* p. 60.

4. Center for Strategic and International Studies, "American Military Culture in the Twenty-first Century: A Report of the CSIS International Security Program" (Washington, D.C.: CSIS, February 2000) pp. 1–2.

Perhaps one of the most striking findings was that almost all—95 percent—of the respondents, from all services and ranks, reported that they were proud to serve in America's armed forces. That is not a small statement. Indeed, among the positions in which the respondents to the survey voiced the strongest agreement on this issue, were:

★ "If necessary to accomplish a combat/lifesaving mission I am ready to put my life on the line . . ."
★ "The armed forces have a right to expect high standards of me when I am off-duty as well as on-duty . . ."
★ "I have a deep personal commitment and a strong desire to serve the nation as a member of the armed forces . . ."

The results were not all rosy. Respondents expressed a great deal of concern about a number of quality-of-life issues, including pay, operational tempo (how often individuals have to leave home to engage in missions for significant periods of time), stress level, and the "zero defect" mentality in the services (i.e., one mistake and you're fired). They were concerned about the availability of adequate material resources to accomplish their missions and were concerned that their superiors were unwilling to allow bad news to flow up the chain of command. Yet despite these and other real practical concerns, service members see tremendous value in what they do and rate their military culture more highly than civilians rate the civilian world.

A recent study concluded that individuals find the nonmaterial benefits of military service the most compelling reason to stay when they reenlist. Some critics of the current military refer to it as a "mercenary force." In the words of researcher John Farris: "Most career-oriented officers make their decision to remain in the military despite perceptions of economic loss. Much more significant in determining career plans are the satisfactions of the military work role, and the relationship with co-workers and supervisors [or what the military calls camaraderie]."[5] Indeed, in the *Military City* poll, the number one reason that poll takers gave for remaining in the military was patriotism.

ANTIWAR, PRO-MILITARY SERVICE

Members of the military have a range of views about any war they are asked to fight, including, of course, the conflicts in Afghanistan and Iraq. What is significant is that many in the military family who are against America's involvement in Iraq remain in favor of military service.

Historian Andrew Bacevich has published his arguments against the war in Iraq in newspapers, magazines, and a book, *The New American Militarism*. But his son serves in the Army. How does Professor Bacevich feel about this? "The word proud does not begin to express how I feel about my son," he says. "But although President Bush is my son's commander-in-chief, my son does not serve the president. He serves us—the American people. Regardless of whether someone has qualms about politics, the important and really admirable thing is to serve the larger community. Given the level of partisanship and personal animus in politics today, there's a lot of confusion on this issue. My own view is that whatever one thinks of a president or his policies, serving the nation remains just about the most admirable thing a citizen can do."[6]

Paul Reickhoff, head of Operation Truth, a group that seeks to provide the unfiltered views of those serving in Iraq, has been a critic

---

5. Michael C. Densch, "Explaining the Gap" in *Soldiers and Civilians,* p. 293, quoted. Densch quotes John H. Farris "Economic and Non-economic Factors of Personnel Recruitment and Retention in the AVF," *Armed Forces and Society* 10 (Winter) 25.
6. Andrew Bacevich, interviewed by Kathryn Roth-Douquet, July 22, 2005.

of many aspects of that war. As he says, he had "reservations about the rationale for the war, about the way it was conceived and executed. We were left without a plan and had to make it up on our own." At the same time, Reickhoff notes that he is still in the Reserves. He says he, "loves the Army, loves the infantry. And at this point I have so much knowledge it would be wrong for me to leave. I would recommend military service to others. Not everybody's cut out for the military. That's not a bad thing. But I developed tremendously, and I think I'm a better person for being involved. The mammoth size of the challenge you take on as a combat leader is bigger than anything else you can do."[7]

Frank has probably have received as much mail and e-mail from the military family as any civilian in the country outside of the White House or Congress. In particular, his file of letters is probably more extensive that anyone else's when it comes to letters from the parents, wives, husbands, and children of military people.

In this voluminous correspondence, military people expressing a strongly positive feeling about what they or their family members do outnumber people who express negative feelings, literally by more than a hundred to one. It is worth noting that the articles and books by Frank that military people were responding to were far from an exercise in military boosterism. For instance, *Faith of Our Sons* is a book about the heart-wrenching experience of sending a son into combat. And a lot of what Frank was writing in the *Washington Post* and other papers such as *USA Today* was about the challenges facing military families, including the stinginess of the death benefits provided to military widows. It was the sort of material that might have been expected to draw out malcontents. One piece Frank wrote was "officially" answered in the *Washington Post* by the head of the

---

7. Paul Reickhoff, interviewed by Kathryn Roth-Douquet, June 15, 2005.

Department of Veterans Affairs, defending it from Frank's attack on the benefits system. Nevertheless, Frank heard from literally thousands of military families who were glad someone was affirming their commitment to service. Many of them said something to the effect that while they had complaints about benefits, nevertheless they were glad they were in the military. And this *included* letters from families of killed or wounded soldiers and Marines.

THE MILITARY MISSION

The virtues many in the military find in their experience derive in part from their mission. Many American civilians have recently seen the U.S. military only in terms of Iraq. But although as we write this book the wars in Iraq and Afghanistan and the War on Terror have been central to the military's mission, they do not define it.

Four-star general (ret.) Anthony Zinni, former combatant commander for the region stretching from the Mediterranean to the Middle East, described his role in the military in one five-year period in the early nineties: "I have trained and established police forces, judiciary committees and judges, and prison systems; I have resettled refugees, in massive numbers, twice; I've negotiated with warlords, tribal leaders, and clan elders; I have distributed food, provided medical assistance, worried about well-baby care, and put in place obstetrical clinics; I've run refugee camps; and I've managed newspapers and run radio stations to counter misinformation attempts."[8]

Former Marine Corps commandant Charles Krulak characterizes the Marine Corps' current mission and combat scenario as a three-block war—where a Marine may separate warring combatants in one block, cradle a baby on the second block, and fire at an attacking enemy on the third block.

---

8. Quoted in Thomas E. Ricks, *Making the Corps* (New York: Touchstone, 1997) p. 186.

The U.S. divides up the world into five regions. Each has a combatant commander, formerly known as commander in chief, with a staff that initiates ongoing interactions and contingency plans for anything that might happen—on the theory that once a need to respond arises, it will be time for action and too late to plan our response.

The U.S. military today is in nearly 130 countries across the globe. Its missions range from combat operations, to peacekeeping, to humanitarian operations, to training foreign troops. It pursues activities that may once have been the bailiwick of the State Department, the Agency for International Development (AID), or other agencies, taken on in the face of dwindling funding for those other agencies. It carries on political science research and study. Some military members spend twenty years involved in academic research and teaching.

In recent years members of the U.S. military have saved hundreds of thousands from certain starvation in Africa, and hundreds of thousands more from ethnic cleansing in Central Europe. In 2005, 350,000 U.S. troops were deployed worldwide. In the summer of 2005, 150,000 troops were in Iraq and Afghanistan. Here is how U.S. Army General John Abizaid, Commanding Officer of Central Command, the region that includes the Middle East, characterized them[9]:

> The young men and women serving in Iraq, Afghanistan, across the Middle East, and throughout the world during this ongoing War on Terror are already making a generational mark. . . . In their selfless service, the over one million young American men and women who have braved the daily dangers

---

9. This paraphrase was provided to us by members of General Abizaid's speechwriting staff; it is a compilation from several speeches the general gave in late 2004 and early 2005.

posed by the Taliban in Afghanistan, Zarqawi's terrorist and Baathist-rejectionist insurgents in Iraq, and the disciples of al Qaida and its radical ideology in places from Morocco to the Philippines have demonstrated the courage of commitment and the will to protect American freedoms and democracy and to assist in the spread of human freedoms and democratic ideals around the globe.

Without protest or complaint, this generation's military volunteers and their families have shouldered the responsibilities of America's freedom and are helping to advance the freedoms of nearly a billion people across the greater Middle East. In the process of honoring their civic duty to our nation, the graduates of Harvard, Yale, Princeton, or Stanford should take note. These volunteers and their families display daily the skills that will make them the political and social force to be reckoned with in our country's future. . . .

Because they have experienced what it is to sacrifice self to help advance the great causes of our time, freedom and liberty, these veterans have earned the respect to make the decisions necessary to keep this nation great for generations to come.

The scope of the U.S. military mission continues to grow. In many instances it is hardly covered by the media. Yet, "without protest or complaint, this generation's military volunteers" continue to do their jobs.

The military continues to maintain its mission defending the demilitarized zone (DMZ) in Korea as part of a UN mandate. We have other missions and forward bases that have continued for fifty years in Japan and Germany. But we are also in the Horn of Africa, for antiterrorist operations as well as conducting civil affairs and humanitarian operations—building structures for local populations in Djibouti and Kenya, providing humanitarian assistance in smaller

villages in Djibouti. The U.S. military is elsewhere in Africa, helping to train a number of coastal countries to protect themselves and
their assets and infrastructure from offshore terrorist attacks, particularly their oil platforms, and their ships, which are harassed by
pirates.

Current U.S. missions include patrolling the Mediterranean Sea
as part of NATO, to help defend against potential terrorist attacks
and to maintain stability in the whole region. The Air National
Guard patrols U.S. skies every day, particularly over New York City
and Washington, D.C. About twenty-six bases around the country
now have fighters armed and ready to scramble at ten minutes' notice in response to any future 9/11 type of situation. The Coast Guard
has become the front line of defense of many ports and facilities
against acts of terror.

From the Coral Sea to the Mediterranean, the U.S. military, in
conjunction with other nations, is conducting exercises to interdict
banned chemicals and other materials intended for the use in prolif-
erate chemical, biological, and nuclear weapons. This initiative began
in 2003 and has resulted, for instance, in the confiscation of phospho-
rus pentasulphide shipped from North Korea.[10]

Americans tend to remember Somalia only in terms of the tragedy of the eighteen service members killed by a Somali mob. What is
often forgotten is that we ended a famine, literally saving the lives of
hundreds of thousands of people, in a spectacular and unparalleled
humanitarian success. We ended wars and sectarian violence in Bosnia and Kosovo. The world would look very different if not for our
intervention there. The relief effort in Pakistan after the 2005 earthquake has depended on U.S. forces.

Most military people have participated in missions where they've
seen positive results. They know they have the ability to affect the

---

10. *Christian Science Monitor,* August 12, 2003.

world, and the skill and ethics that they bring to their work make a difference. And they understand their service to be indispensable. One refrain we hear again and again from military people is that as they traveled the world to various troubled places, they came to see the American role in a new light. As a result some feel that Americans who have not shared the experience just don't "get" what the real world consists of, and what it would look like in our absence.

CHARACTER AND SERVICE

Most veterans credit the lessons they learned in the military with enabling much of their subsequent success. For instance, Louis Giuliano, the recently retired chairman of ITT Industries and a former Army first lieutenant, says that the military teaches the responsibility of serving, not just fulfilling your own needs. Chairman of Hill and Knowlton USA Thomas Hogg, a former naval aviator, says, "Everything I know about leadership, I learned in the military."[11]

Many books have been written on the leadership methods developed by our military and copied, often enviously, by American business and academic communities. In *Business Leadership the Marine Corps Way,* by Dan Carrison and Rod Walsh, two former Marines, one a senior account executive for Diebold and the other president of Blue-Chip Inventory Service, show that the methods of recruitment, basic training, supervision, and instilling organizational leadership skills are better and more productive in the Marine Corps than in most American businesses. They also list former Marines who have been presidents or CEOs of top American companies, including the *New York Times,* Campbell Soup, CBS Productions, Chase Manhattan Bank, the Chrysler Corporation, Equitable Life Insurance

---

11. Del Jones, "A Vanishing Breed: CEOs Seasoned by Military Combat," *USA Today,* January 2005, p. 1B.

Society, Exxon Corp., First National Bank, the Ford Motor Company, *Fortune* magazine, the General Motors Corporation, Merrill Lynch, Morgan Guaranty Trust, and Time Inc.

The authors conclude that successful businesses have to somehow try to teach what the military takes for granted: an ethic of service, teamwork, and selflessness without which any great endeavor becomes impossible.[12] And of course the Army, Navy, Air Force, and Coast Guard have their own impressive lists of alumni.

Many men and women in the military provide a benefit to our society beyond the "official" contribution they make as our defenders. In fact we have talked with many a recruiter and drill instructor who understands his or her role as twofold: first, to recruit and train America's defenders, but second and no less important, to make good citizens.

DEMOGRAPHICS—WHO SERVES IN THE MILITARY TODAY

The images of the high school dropout or recent convict who chose the Army rather than jail is outdated. In 2003, the *New York Times* reported demographic statistics that show the working class and the middle class provide the bulk of recruits. A number of other studies have found the same. As the *Times* piece shows, most of our military people come from solid working-class and middle-class homes. New recruits are also increasingly second-generation military. Perhaps this is natural—the sons and daughters of lawyers become lawyers, the children of bricklayers are often bricklayers. So, too, do the offspring of soldiers grow up to wear a uniform.

There is a regional flavor to those who serve. Fewer come from the Northeast and big cities. The majority comes from the Midwest

---

12. Dan Carrison and Rod Walsh, *Business Leadership the Marine Corps Way* (New York: Barnes & Noble Books, 1999) pp. 10–15.

and the South. They strongly identify as Christian, and Roman Catholics edge out Evangelical Protestants in surveys, somewhat against stereotype. There are other things that may surprise people unfamiliar with the military. Education is very important. More than a quarter of career enlisted have a college degree. Officers are required to have a college degree to qualify for their commission, of course. But for officers at mid-career and above, graduate work is the norm.[13] James A. Davis, a former Harvard professor of sociology and researcher at the National Opinion Research Center, looked at the education, religion, class background, and regional origin of more-senior officers.[14] He found that almost all of these officers had done graduate work, and three-quarters held at least one graduate degree. It is common for officers to hold two graduate degrees.

ROTC cadets do better than the general civilian college population on standardized tests: the average SAT score for ROTC cadets was 1250 at a time when the civilian average was 900.[15]

The military is not as predictable politically as some people may think either. Although most members of the military consider themselves both Republican and conservative, when questioned on actual policy positions, there are areas in which members of the military are actually more liberal than the general population.

For instance, in the Davis study, more-senior officers were "as

---

13. "Field grade" officers and above, or majors through generals and their Navy counterparts, lieutenant commanders through admirals. The military services have number designations for each of the ranks, beginning with the letter O for officers, then 1 for second lieutenant, 2 for first, 3 for captain, 4 for major, 5 for lieutenant colonel, 6 for colonel, 7 and up for the general categories. Because of history and tradition, the Navy has the same ranks structure—O1 through the O7+ ranks, but they call them by different names. The majority of the survey, about 70 percent, comprised the lower two field-grade ranks—majors/lieutenant commanders and lieutenant colonels/commanders.

14. James A. Davis, "Attitudes and Opinions Among Senior Military Officers and a U.S. Cross-Section, 1998–1999," in *Soldiers and Civilians*, p. 101.

15. Densch, "Explaining the Gap," p. 295, quoting William P. Snyder, "Officer Recruitment for the All-Volunteer Force," *Armed Forces and Society*, 10 (Spring) 410–411.

liberal as liberals and Democrats on social matters, and as conservative as Republicans on economic matters." In comparison with most
U.S. adults, upper-grade military officers are unambiguously more
tolerant of free speech (in the survey, this meant keeping books on
atheism, communism, and homosexuality in the library), less upset
about declining morals and the decline of traditional values, and
more likely to favor "think for themselves" than "obedience" as a
value that should be imparted to children.

But what about the junior enlisted person, what the public thinks
of as the grunt? (Although being a "grunt"—in the infantry—is
only one of many possible jobs.) Here, too, it is Middle America that
is overrepresented.[16] There are slight differences from the general
population that make the young people who currently enlist less
likely to be white, more likely to be from single-parent working-class
families, but researchers concluded that deviations are so small, that
in fact the enlisted population of the military resemble the American
working class in general.[17] The typical American soldier or sailor
comes from a small farm community or is the son of a car mechanic
in a small town. His or her mom may be a single parent, but it is
unlikely that she is on welfare. More typically she will be a nurse or
work in a factory.

Children of officers and NCOs (noncommissioned officers—
those who lead within the enlisted ranks) are six times more likely to
make the military their career.[18] Today the average enlisted soldier

16. David R. Segal, Peter Freedman-Doan, Jerald G. Bachman, and Patrick M. O'Malley,
"Attitudes of Entry-Level Enlisted Personnel," in *Soldiers and Civilians,* p. 163.
17. Segal et al., using data from the Monitoring the Future project, conducted by the Survey Research Center from the University of Michigan. The study involved approximately
17,000 male high school seniors each year from 1976 to 1995, with follow-up surveys conducted every several years. David R. Segal, Peter Freedman-Doan, Jerald G. Bachman,
and Patrick M. O'Malley, "Attitudes of Entry-Level Enlisted Personnel: Pro-Military
and Politically Mainstream," in Feaver and Kohn, *Soldiers and Civilians,* p. 174.
18. Farris, 1981, pp. 550–554.

serves more than seven years, which contrasts with the "two-years-and-out" pattern of the military draftee in previous eras of service.

John McCain, senator and former prisoner of war, is one of the most widely admired figures in American public life. He addressed the young men and women at the U.S. Naval Academy on October 9, 2001—two days after the bombing of Afghanistan began—recalling his own experiences. It seems to us that he articulated what most people we know in the military family believe about service:

> Soon you will be the shield behind which marches the enduring message of our revolution. There is no greater duty, no greater honor. . . . Hold that honor as dearly as your country holds you. Hold it as dearly as do those who have already been called to the battle. Hold it as if it were your greatest treasure. Because it is. It is. Whatever sacrifices you must bear, you will know a happiness far more sublime than pleasure. My warrior days were long ago, but not so long ago that I have forgotten their purpose and their reward.[19]

While many in the American elite might admire the poetry of Mc-Cain's words, his ideas would seem exotic to them. To men and women in the military, John McCain describes the reality they know and feel honored to be part of.

---

19. Connie Bruck, "McCain's Party," *The New Yorker,* May 30, 2005.

4. The Emergence of the Gap

★ ★ ★ ★ ★ ★ ★ ★ ★ ★ ★ ★ ★ ★

It may be laid down as a primary position, and the basis of our system, that every Citizen who enjoys the protection of a Free Government owes not only a proportion of his property, but even of his personal services, to the defense of it.

—George Washington

The concept of a "gap" between the military and society, even elite society, would have been nonsensical to most people in this nation's history. Until the late 1960s serving in the military was for many men an incident of life, a matter of course. But aside from the Revolutionary War and the Civil War, mass mobilization was rare in our early history. American women, most of whom did not see active duty, were also involved for periods of time: if their husbands, sons, and fathers served, the women ran farms, maintained businesses, raised families, and made ends meet in the meantime. The phrase "They who wait also serve" was true then, as now.

The potential need for individuals to participate in their country's military service was a fact of life that was understood as inevitable, as part of being a member of an increasingly important nation in a complex world. Civilian and soldier were simply different aspects of the same person. The need for the military was not questioned.

Patriotism itself was a self-evident virtue, rooted in the individual's belief in the nobility of the American experiment in democracy. This belief had deep theological roots in our country, which, as many observers have noted, was religious from its foundation. There are important caveats here—the moral issue of slavery caused many to object to national military goals in the early nineteenth century (in order to prevent slavery's spread). And questions have always been asked about the morality of every war our country has ever fought. Pacifism, usually with religious roots, is not a new idea. But nevertheless, a certain broad level of commitment to the national enterprise was taken for granted.

Today, in contrast, civilian and soldier are frequently seen as different beasts. As a reporter who was recently embedded with an artillery battalion in Iraq described himself and his encounter with the Marines, he was like "a cat looking at penguins."[1] To this reporter, these Americans in uniform were creatures so different from him as to be truly "other," and the Marines saw him likewise. How did we get here?

Frank

I see this question—how did we get from "us" to "them" in terms of the military—through the lens of my own family's experience. A year or two after John joined the Corps I wanted to learn about our family military history. I started to press my mother and my wife,

---

1. Chris Ayers, interviewed on "Morning Edition," NPR, August 30, 2005.

Genie, and her sister Pam for Schaeffer and Walsh clan military history. I'd never bothered to think about our family's military past. Did we have one?

We did indeed have a military history, but in the space of a generation it was almost forgotten. At one time most everyone had served. Now out of our expanded Walsh and Schaeffer families, dozens and dozens of us, one lone son had donned a uniform.

My mother's ancestors (Merritts and Sevilles) fought in the American Revolution and the Civil War on the Union side. My grandfather on my father's side (a second-generation German immigrant) ran away to sea when he was twelve, joined the U.S. Navy, trained on the *Constellation*—"When the ships were made of wood and men were made of iron," as he used to tell my dad—and fought in the Spanish-American War.

My father did not fight in World War II, but as a pastor worked tirelessly in relief efforts for young people in bombed-out European cities right after the war. He had an active-duty relationship with the U.S. military and traveled on a military pass through Europe while working with U.S. military commanders in various occupied cities, helping the English, German, French, Dutch, and Italian populations recover.

Genie's parents, Stan and Betty Walsh, were definitely members of the "greatest generation." Stan's family had been homesteaders in western North Dakota in the early 1900s. Stan grew up in the Great Depression and went to the University of North Dakota, arriving with one pair of shoes and fifteen dollars in his pocket. Stan spent the first year living in a converted railroad caboose with five other students.

At Georgetown Law School, Stan was too poor to buy books; he completed his law studies using the Library of Congress books he was able to borrow because of the kindness of one of his state's senators. Stan served in the Coast Guard during the war, in spite of having had a very serious injury to his arm that should have kept him out. In fact, he essentially lied and begged his way into serving. It was simply not considered honorable to stand by while others served in a time of war.

Stan married Betty King, who first worked for the FBI, then the Coast Guard as a SPAR, assigned to the encoding unit. (She packed a forty-five almost as big as herself while carrying top-secret documents from one office to another in Norfolk, Virginia.) Betty's ancestors had fought in the American Revolution; one of them was a signatory of the Constitution.

After the war Stan became a successful San Francisco lawyer, practiced and taught law, and raised a family of five. Almost all the students he taught in law school were there on the G.I. Bill, and when they came over to their young professor's home for a meal, they met as former soldiers and Marines who had all been in uniform not long before.

Genie's older brother, Tom, served in the Army during the Vietnam War. He volunteered. Then out of all twelve Walsh grandchildren, only John Schaeffer volunteered. On my side of the family none of my siblings served, nor did I, and out of my parents' twenty-three grandchildren and great-grandchildren only John volunteered.

The Walsh clan mostly voted Democrat. My parents voted Republican. But we were all part of a class that had moved "beyond" service. With all those college degrees and the upward mobility, the idea of military service had been abandoned. Just for the record, I would never have had to go to Vietnam, though I was just possibly old enough by the end of that war. I'd had polio as a two-year-old, and my atrophied left leg would have kept me out of the military even if I had begged to get in—which I did not.

It turned out that from the perspective of family history, John's service was normal. It was only to me and to my generation and our children that it might appear strange to have a son serving his country. It was never spoken out loud, but the assumption was that one's children didn't need to do anything to earn citizenship other than get good grades and then a good job as fast as possible. On that issue, the Roman Catholic, liberal Democrat Walsh clan and the Protestant evangelical, conservative Republican Schaeffers were agreed—not that we ever thought to discuss it.

Kathy

My family is relatively new to America compared to Frank's. My parents are both first-generation Americans, and prior to emigrating both sides of my family lived in places referred to generically and darkly as "the Old Country," places where Jews did best to stay out of the way of the authorities as much as possible. There are a lot of rabbis and furniture salesmen in my family tree, but not many soldiers.

My father, however, was drafted in the early sixties and did a two-and-a-half-year stint for the Air Force, as a pediatrician at Strategic Air Command bases in Morocco and Spain. It was a good adventure for my parents, as I understand it, something that my father was asked to do, and did because he was asked, without reserve or regret. He enjoyed his time in service and developed a respect for the military from it.

As it happened, I was born on one of those bases. My father's Air Force commitment ended when I was a few weeks old, and we returned to the States, where my father resumed his medical residency and the military experience receded into the past.

I didn't return to a military base until nineteen years later, in 1983, the summer after my first year at college. I went for a weekend with my friend Lisa to the Seneca Women's Peace Encampment in upstate New York, and got myself arrested at an Army depot there. I was a tourist, really, in it for the experience. Getting arrested was the purpose of the trip; it was what people did at the Peace Encampment.

We got arrested because the Seneca Army Depot, abutting Romulus, New York, was stockpiling nuclear weapons, and we were there to protest those nuclear weapons. The depot was also adjacent to the town of Seneca Falls, where the landmark women's suffrage convention was held in the nineteenth century, thus we got a twofer—pro-women and no-nukes.

The camp was like a kids' summer camp, spread out in some fields at the edge of the woods, in muggy air whose smell conjures up school vacation for me to this day. We slept in raised wooden cabins on cots, communally ate the food that was cooked by a rotating group of assignees, and participated in an elaborate representative/consensus–based decision making that even in my wide-eyed years I lacked the patience for.

The first day, I joined a group that was organized for a foray into town to buy groceries and win the hearts and minds of the locals. Somehow I got the sense that the locals had had more than enough of us at that point. When we got to the town square, some of the townspeople were there apparently waiting, and they crowded around us, yelling loudly, their faces red. One of the more popular expressions I heard in Romulus was, "Go home, you lezzie bitches."

There were in fact a healthy number of lesbians at the camp, and there was a much-publicized controversy at the camp about whether or not to fly an American flag for July Fourth, all of which stirred up a lot of emotion in Romulus. Still, the intensity of the anger surprised me.

Then the next day we trained, and practiced, and climbed over the fence at the Army depot. Our purpose, I suppose, was to log our displeasure with the nuclear weapons that were being held there. In theory, we would go to the weapons and take hammers to them, beating swords into plowshares. We knew, however, that our activities would end when we crossed the fence, that the military police would be there to arrest us. We were given the option to go limp, in good conscientious-objector fashion, or not.

There were a whole lot of us climbing the fence. It is awkward climbing a chain-link fence, your tennis shoe has to wedge into the bottom part of the diamond made by the metal wire links. We had ratty beach towels to drape over the barbed wire, for when we were to swing ourselves over the top. Even more women watched us go, cheering us on. The military police, young, nicely scrubbed men and women, waited patiently for us to come over. Unlike the townspeople, they seemed not to be bothered by us. On the ground, I heard one of the women protesters complain loudly that the MPs were hurting her, but when I glanced over I didn't see anything incriminating. The two who attended to me were relaxed. I went limp. Having gone to the trouble to participate in the first place, I thought it was worth doing it all the way. I remember telling my MPs I was sorry for making them have to drag me to the bus—it suddenly struck me that it didn't seem fair that they took the brunt of this. They genially assured me that they didn't mind.

It was a little embarrassing, despite all our rhetoric about the bravery of civil disobedience. Our action had the elaborate and predictable feel of Kabuki theater, with the Army folks as forced participants. That same day, we were processed and let go. Day three, I went home.

I got a sense of a lot of truths about the country during that weekend. One of them had to do with the equanimity with which the military received us. We didn't bother or offend them; we were just part of the American experience, I guess. Another was how the townspeople perceived us—I had thought of us as a benign presence to them—after all, did they want nuclear warheads in their backyard, didn't that make their lives scarier? I hadn't taken into account that the base brought money into an otherwise depressed area. And I didn't understand that the locals were proud of the people who served on the base, and that we were an affront to the townspeople, that some of them probably had sons or daughters in the military.

The purpose of our civil disobedience was not to actually accomplish a strategic end (though organizers did hope that protests like ours would spring up worldwide and force the end of nuclear weapons). The immediate purpose was self-expression. We had come of age in a world where self-expression was an important right, perhaps even *the* important right, certainly more important in our eyes than any property rights the government might have.

Nonetheless, the MPs did not seem to begrudge us our rights. That was perhaps my first inkling of the relationship between individual members of the military and the Constitution.

Needless to say, this kind of protest would not have been conceivable pre-Vietnam, which is not to say that there were not antiwar protesters before. There is a long history of idealism and activism, much of which is honorable. But it rarely involved tourists.

Before Vietnam middle-class students like me, lacking any firm conviction about the issue, would not have so easily felt that breaking the law on a military base (as absent of repercussions as that in fact was) was a perfectly acceptable thing to do. The formula that imagined the powerless but conscientious individual speaking up to authority in a heroic light had not taken its full expression until the seventies. It was the imagined glow of that ideal that made our action seem reasonable in 1983.

Kathy and Frank

America was founded by farmers, statesmen, and bankers who were military men when circumstances called for it. George Washington, Thomas Jefferson, James Madison and others did not want a country with a military culture, but they expected their countrymen to serve the nation when needed.

The drafters of the Constitution cared deeply about America's military. They gave more attention to military affairs than to any other aspect of government, seventeen constitutional clauses in all.[2] Perhaps the single theme that most ties together the framers' intent for the armed forces was that it be firmly connected to the citizenry. To that end, control of the military is divided between the two main elected bodies, the Congress and the president. A citizen military— the militia (known today as the National Guard)—was seen as an important component of our defense. The militia and the Second Amendment together suggest America's founders pictured a country in which men, in general, would have fundamental military skills and participate in at least some military activities.[3]

Perhaps wary of the authoritarian role that the British military had played on U.S. soil, the early political view in this country was against a standing army and staunchly in favor of the citizen-soldier, the individual who had a regular civilian life and commitment— perhaps a farm to run—which he left at times of his country's need.[4]

America was leery of creating the kind of warrior caste that developed in European nations such as Prussia most especially from the time of Frederick the Great forward, which could have an effect

---

2. We are indebted to Professor Donald N. Zillman for his excellent analysis of the armed forces in the Constitution, in "Where Have All the Soldiers Gone?"
3. Ibid.
4. This was the position of the Democratic-Republican Party, founded by Thomas Jefferson, and under whose banner Jefferson and later James Madison, James Monroe, and Andrew Jackson, among others, held the presidency. This broad-based notion of the American soldier squared with the active 19th-century use of the American military, to hold the claim on the newly purchased Louisiana Territories, to defend against the British in the War of 1812, to secure the noninvolvement of Europe in Western Hemisphere affairs under the Monroe Doctrine, and to squelch South Carolina's early threat of secession in the 1830s.

on the country's foreign policy. This was part of a general suspicion of all elite-led castes. There was also a strong sense that the manifest destiny of America was to allow its citizens the freedom to pursue individual dreams free from government intrusion.

But George Washington and others who warned against the dangers of a standing military did not warn against a citizen performing military duty. They considered it a point of pride and honor for an individual to serve. And even the most democratic of the founders, Thomas Jefferson, wanted an educated and professional officer corps. To this end he founded the West Point military academy.

Throughout the country's history, the story of military service has been a story of "plus-up" during crisis, and "draw-down" in the immediate aftermath of peace. The country always maintained a navy and a Marine Corps, which were small and handled smaller political and policing missions. This continued until the mid-twentieth century.

For most of this time, American citizens moved in and out of military duty when called on, regardless of party and less constrained by class than today. The leaders of society in every war boasted sons in uniform, even though, human nature being what it is, there were undoubtedly some who used privilege to avoid duty.

America used conscription in the Civil War, World War I, and from 1940 until the end of the Vietnam War. The country always had a high percentage of volunteers in the Army, Navy, and Marines (and later, the Air Force). A large proportion of the population would serve when called. Thus, in the War of 1812, over a quarter of the eligible men were mobilized.[5] In the Mexican War, from 1846 to 1847, roughly a tenth of the eligible men fought.[6]

---

5. A total of 286,000 troops fought that war when the country's population was little over 1 million white men between the ages 16 and 44.
6. This totaled 79,000 troops, drawn from a population that had 850,000 men aged 20 to 39.

At the beginning of the Civil War, in 1861, President Lincoln asked for 75,000 volunteers, and he quickly received all the men necessary. College professors served, as did wealthy and educated men, such as Louisa May Alcott's father, who helped with the wounded. Sons from the wealthiest and most humble families fought. The poet Walt Whitman volunteered as a nurse.

Ultimately, over 2.2 million troops fought in the Civil War, at a time when the population of white male twenty-to-twenty-nine-year-olds was a bit over 2.46 million.[7] It's a staggering figure, and brings home the universality of the military experience.

In 1863 America had a debilitating experience with conscription. The North instituted a draft with two terribly ill-conceived opt-out provisions—one could pay $300 to avoid service or one could hire a volunteer to go in the draftee's place. This led to the slogan, "rich man's fight, but a poor man's war," and contributed to anti-conscription riots among urban workers. The opt-out provisions—not the draft itself—undermined morale and the legitimacy of the fight by allowing the wealthy to avoid service, while asking those with less means to serve. America learned its lessons, at least for the next hundred years.

The military drew down after the Civil War, increasing again thirty years later for the Spanish-American War in 1898. About 300,000 troops participated in that war, out of a population that had grown. There were then 14 million white men between eighteen and forty-four years old. That war lasted less than a year, and after it was over the services drew down again.

It was another twenty years before the next generation of Americans was asked to fight. In World War I, 4.7 million Americans fought, a figure equal to about one-sixth of all the men (32.3 million) over the

---

7. Population figures from the 1860 census. Civil War troop levels taken from a chart of historical operations on globalsecurity.org. "19th Century Operations," http://www.globalsecurity.org/military/ops/19cent-ops.htm.

children in uniform. . . . James, Elliott, John, and Franklin Jr. [Roosevelt] saw action. Randolph Churchill [Winston's son] would be under fire in different theaters and sustained injuries, and his sisters, Diana, Sarah, and Mary, were in uniform, Mary manning an antiaircraft battery in London and later in north-west Europe. [Roosevelt's adviser Harry] Hopkins' sons, Robert and Stephen, served. Stephen would die in the Pacific. . . . This human dimension of Roosevelt's and Churchill's wartime lives has largely been forgotten, but the safety of their children was always on their minds, and they often asked after each other's broods. Eleanor recalled, 'Both of them [Roosevelt and Churchill] would have liked to have taken their sons' places.' . . . Those pins [marking the position of troops] in the map rooms, from London to Washington, had faces attached to them—and some of those faces were their own children's.[11]

There was more to be gained by widespread participation in the military besides simply egalitarian good feeling. With all classes being represented came a higher level of accountability and innovation. Victor Davis Hanson argues in *Carnage and Culture: Landmark Battles in the Rise of Western Power* that "none outside the West drafted fighters with the implicit understanding that their military service was part and parcel of their status as free citizens who were to determine when, how, and why they were to go to war."[12] Hanson makes a strong case for the fact that it was this aspect of a "citizen military" that contributed mightily to American military successes. Mixing all classes made the process democratic, and therefore put the military's

---

11. Jon Meacham, *Franklin and Winston: An Intimate Portrait of an Epic Friendship* (New York: Random House, 2003) p. 176.
12. Victor Davis Hanson, *Carnage and Culture: Landmark Battles in the Rise of Western Power* (New York: Doubleday, 2001) p. 455.

actions and tactics under a level of scrutiny and accountability unknown in non-Western nations. We argue that it is this traditional source of strength that we are undermining today with our largely class-bound military.

Until just after the war, 1946, applicants for U.S. citizenship were required to promise military service before they would be admitted to citizenship. Failure to promise was considered a sign of bad character and lack of attachment to the principles of the Constitution. The Supreme Court overturned this practice but presumed that the new citizen would embrace other ways to participate in any potential war effort. As Supreme Court justice William O. Douglas reasoned, "The annals of the recent war show that many whose religious scruples prevented them from bearing arms, nevertheless were unselfish participants in the war effort."[13]

In other words, as long as the new Americans who might be pacifists for religious reasons, such as the Seventh-Day Adventists (who were well known for their bravery as medics on the battlefield), evinced a willingness to serve in the military in noncombatant roles, they were still to be considered worthy citizens. It was assumed, however, that a disinclination to serve at all—and remember, there was no war in 1946—would disqualify any man from deserving citizenship. One could not claim full citizenship in 1946 and say at the same time that one simply had "other priorities" than serving.[14]

America's role in the world as a great power expanded exponentially after World War II. It was then, in the 1950s, for the first time in its history, that America developed a large standing army. For the

---

13. *Girouard v. U.S.*, 328 U.S. 61(1946).

14. Vice President Richard Cheney explained the eleven deferments he sought and received from the Vietnam draft as simply a matter of having "other priorities" than military service at that time in his life. Quoted in interview by George C. Wilson in the *Washington Post*, 1989, as quoted by Timothy Noah "How Dick Cheney is like Dan Quayle," *Slate*, July 27, 2000 at http://www.slate.com/id/1005761/.

first thirty-odd years of America's leadership in the world, for the period just preceding World War II and until the end of the Vietnam War in 1973, the United States staffed its large armed forces with volunteers and with conscripts, also known as draftees. This standing army was also what is called a mass army—one that is drawn from all of society.

The Soviet challenge after the end of World War II precluded the traditional stand-down in the eyes of policy makers on both the Left and the Right. After the Cold War, America did draw down, only to find herself with unparalleled responsibilities for maintaining world order. The military services all expressed concerns in the interwar decade of the nineties about how thin their troops were spread. Nations might complain about American "hegemony," but as was seen in the crisis in the Balkans, whenever real trouble brewed the cry went up on all sides: Where are the Americans? Why don't they *do* something?

One residual result of the era when all classes served was that up until the 1990s, veterans were overrepresented in Congress (in percentage terms more congressmen had military experience than did the general public). It was considered very appropriate that those who would lead would first serve, "pay their dues," particularly when they might eventually craft policy that would send another generation of Americans into harm's way.

Americans recognized on some level that military service confers a special claim to full citizenship. Therefore black Americans viewed their exclusion from the military and then their segregation into noncombat roles as discriminatory. It was not for nothing that black military men marched triumphantly through Harlem after returning from World War I, where an all-black regiment had distinguished itself with great honor in combat.

For the same reasons the feminists of the late '60s and early '70s fought to expand the role of women in the military (and many continue to try to expand women's combat roles). And today, the gays-in-the-military debate includes the same rhetoric.

"For the generations that fought the Civil War and the world wars, and even those who served in the 1950s and 1960s," according to Andrew Bacevich, "citizenship and military service remained intimately connected."[15] Military service, in other words, was not the province of a few, but rather of all. A whole class of people simply opting out would have been mocked as an act of cowardice and proof of a lack of commitment to the country and to one's fellows.

MODERN ERA

World War I was devastating. More men—American, British, French, and German—were killed in a single week of battle than died on the American side in the whole Vietnam War. There was a great flowering of literature during and after that war, much of it steeped in modern ideas of cosmopolitanism and distrust of authority and the traditions that had apparently failed to prevent an insane bloodletting.

Much of the literary reaction—from *All Quiet on the Western Front* to *Mrs. Dalloway* to the poems of Wilfred Owen—combined the ideas that war is horrible and that authority is not to be trusted. We point this out not to critique these books or poems—they are important literature. But the fact is that for a whole generation of readers their vision of military service was formed by the anti-military and antiwar literature that was the natural reaction to the slaughter of World War I. The overwhelming evil of our opponents in World War II held that perspective at bay for some years. But as "the good war" receded, this literature shaped a lot of people's idea of service in our most educated circles. And to the extent that the

---

15. Bacevich, *New American Militarism,* p. 27.

antiwar books spawned in the period after World War I (not to mention a lot of anti-military post–Vietnam War literature) continue to be read in high school and college English classes, and they continue to be influential.

When art took war as a subject in the twentieth century, it more directly and graphically than ever before rebuked earlier depictions of war-fighting as heroic, and instead furthered the concept that military service was degrading and inhumane. The military was portrayed as part of the problem impeding human development, not part of the solution when force might be needed to stop barbarism or shape history while protecting national interests. And the military was routinely satirized. For instance many of the post–World War I German Expressionists, such as Max Beckmann, George Grosz, and Otto Dix, portrayed the military as the boorish enemy of progress, gross and always somehow linked to profiteering by industrialists on the backs of the dead and dying, or as helpless, despairing victims of fate. And this artistic perspective—fully justified by the horrors of World War I—dovetailed with several literary and religious movements into a tsunami of pacifist and/or utopian expression.

THEOLOGY

The traditional pacifist groups—the Quakers and the Seventh-Day Adventists, groups within the larger Christian denominations, as well as some members of the Jewish community—reacted to the First World War with an understandable sense that their darkest prophesies had been vindicated. But there was a second and, in the end, more important theological trend that dovetailed with other social and artistic movements to produce a new, modern view of all aspects of life, including the military.

After the First World War a new method of biblical interpretation came into fashion. Literary principles of textual analysis were used to "demythologize" the Bible. This liberal or "modernist" theological movement—it had started in European universities in the late nineteenth century as a theological expression of Enlightenment rationalism—won the day in the American mainline denominations. For instance, Princeton Theological Seminary went, in less than ten years, from being a staunch bastion of conservative, traditional Presbyterian Protestant orthodoxy to being a theologically liberal school, and fired several professors on the losing side.

Even before World War I, at the end of the nineteenth century, there was a growing acceptance in intellectual and educated circles of Darwin's theory. Evolution seemed to challenge the idea of providential creation. And the discipline of higher criticism claimed human authorship of the Scriptures. These developments led to many of the educated classes losing faith in the old, orthodox certainties, including certain basic assumptions about "God and country" that heretofore had been shared widely by all classes of Americans.

The main point of the modernist theology was the notion that the divine will of God was going to be seen in the secular progress of man on earth rather than in terms of theology, let alone divine intervention. We were to no longer think in terms of good and evil but in terms of progress from a less enlightened state to a more enlightened state. In the future mankind would not only have progressed technologically but morally. We were going to become better people. We would outgrow things like crime and war. In fact we would outgrow the need to have countries. And in that new and better world who would need a military?

The evolutionary view had, therefore, been thrust into the realm of moral progress. A rosy future awaited those who could dismiss old prejudices. In this view, social as well as biological evolution was taking place. In the new theology, old ideas about original sin—in other words the idea that humans are always going to be imperfect and sometimes evil—were dispensed with. Mankind was essentially good and could be perfected with correct social engineering and good ideas. The idea of patriotism—as a needed bulwark against evil, chaos, and aggression—began to seem downright quaint.

New ways would be found to resolve international conflicts with neither generals nor priests. What was called "development" would be the answer to every problem from "solving" the problem of cretinism to solving the problem of war. It was all just a matter of good science.

On May 21, 1922 a famous Manhattan preacher named Harry Emerson Fosdick delivered one of the most important sermons summarizing the embrace of the new theological liberalism. Liberal Christians, he said

> . . . have assimilated as part of the divine revelation the exhilarating insight which these recent generations have given to us, that development is God's way of working out his will. They see that the most desirable elements in human life have come through the method of development. Men's music has developed from the rhythmic noise of beaten sticks until we have in melody and harmony possibilities once undreamed. Men's painting has developed from the crude outlines of the caveman until in line and color we have achieved unforeseen results and possess latent beauties yet unfolded. Men's architecture has developed from the crude huts of primitive man until our cathedrals and business buildings . . . [evolved] Development does seem to be the way in which God works.[16]

---

16. Peter J. Boyer, "The Big Tent," *The New Yorker,* August 22, 2005. We are indebted to Peter J. Boyer for several of the facts of theological history cited herein.

The utopian aspects of liberal theology went somewhat underground after the horrors of Hitler's Germany and Stalin's Soviet Union became common knowledge. In the shadow of Auschwitz and the Gulag it was harder to argue for a future where we would need no armies to stop evil men. But the utopian impulse did not lose its hold on the imagination of America's educated classes.

LAW

In the mid-twentieth century the Congress and the Supreme Court began carving out more substantive rights for individuals than had ever existed before, leading to an expansion in the legal rights of U.S. citizens.[17] This contributed to a rise in what social scientists call "rights consciousness," meaning the "general awareness of rights to be claimed or asserted against others, particularly the government."[18] As a result, individuals felt they had a right (among other things) not to be forced to go to war; they had a right not to be drafted (although the courts did not agree with them on this point). For the first time, citizens in large part felt fully entitled to their citizenship separate from duty such as military service.

Rights consciousness was energized by the suspicion that the state could easily abuse individuals en masse, and it was a duty of those in good conscience to oppose that official abuse. This was the lesson of the post–World War II Nuremberg trials, where "just following orders" did not serve as a legal excuse for committing atrocities, and

---

17. For instance, the Supreme Court cases of *Goldberg v. Kelly,* 397 U.S. 94(1970), which gave welfare recipients some rights with respect to the government's ability to end those benefits, and *Goss v. Lopez,* 419 U.S. 565(1975), on school disciplinary suspensions.

18. James Burk, "The Military's Presence in American Society, 1950–2000," in *Soldiers and Civilians,* p. 263, also quoting Stephan L. Wasby "History of the Court: Rights Consciousness in Contemporary Society," in *The Oxford Companion to the Supreme Court of the United States,* ed. Kermit L. Hall (New York: Oxford University Press, 1992) p. 398.

therefore one must scrutinize the legitimacy of the orders one's country has issued. This ruling established the principle that individuals can know better than their governments what is right. The civil rights movement further developed this principle, where activists at times broke laws as a matter of conscience to end the oppression of people—in particular, segregation laws that discriminated against black Americans—and were ultimately vindicated by the courts.

TEENAGERS

In other contemporaneous social developments, American society came up with another innovation roughly mid-twentieth century, something new, called a "teenager." Prior to that time, young people did not have a separate status—you were a child or an adult. Now, suddenly, people enjoyed periods of relative freedom, free both of their parents' dominion and of adult responsibilities.[19] Flowering with this freedom and closely related to "rights consciousness" was the ascendance of the idea of the primacy of individual choice made possible by unprecedented levels of wealth and leisure. Enlightened educators and parents sought to allow these citizens of a better future to plot their own life course. And it was this relatively experimental self-conscious teen generation that was asked to fight America's next war, Vietnam.

VIETNAM

Our purpose here is not to refight the Vietnam War but to look at how it created a turning point in the ethics of citizens' participation

---

19. For more on this subject see, e.g., Grace Palladin, *Teenagers: An American History* (Basic Books, New York, 1996). (Arguing teenagers "as a group" did not exist before the 1940s. "But in the fifty years since World War II . . . teenagers have had an enormous impact on American culture.")

in military service. Of course, Vietnam was not the first controversial war in our nation's history. Nor was it the first to use the draft. As we mentioned earlier, there have been drafts for other wars in our nation's history, and continuously from 1940 until the beginning of the current era, when the draft ended in 1973. There were people who did not want to participate in the Civil War and World Wars I and II, not because they were conscientious objectors in a grand moral or religious sense, but because they did not think the war at issue was right or because they just didn't want to be in a dangerous situation. Opposition to those wars never had a broad impact. But social conditions—as previously described—were such in the late '60s and early '70s that opposition to the Vietnam War took a more powerful shape than had any movement's opposition to any war before.

When the Vietnam War began to bog down, there were many who felt it was their right not to fight and many who believed it was an important act of conscience to oppose the war. Never before in American history had the moral certainty with which opponents of the Vietnam War expressed their view been as widespread. And those protesters essentially won—the war ended with a U.S. withdrawal, and the protesters' version of the war is the one that has held the most sway in the post-Vietnam understanding of that period, at least among our educated urban classes. As a result, many of the protesters' premises about the war have remained firmly in place for them as they've aged, and even as certain facts have come to light that might arguably undermine some of the antiwar movement's certainties. For instance, the large scale atrocities committed by the North Vietnamese against those vanquished in the South seem to undermine the rosy vision of the enemy put forward by some protesters.

Hundreds of thousands of people suffered terribly after the Vietcong took over Vietnam, and in ways that are sometimes ignored by people who see the American pullout in terms of universal human rights. Moreover, a certain number of those who dodged the draft simply didn't want to go.

Many who opposed the war saw themselves as right, and therefore more enlightened than other Americans. Yet, there were other people of conscience who believed the war was moral, that it would help America and the democratic cause, and certainly would help the people of South Vietnam. Some of these Americans also saw the Vietnam War in the larger context as part of the Cold War that was being fought to stop the advance of totalitarian communist regimes all over the world, which brought atrocities from the Gulag to Cuba, from Mao's China to North Korea. Some of these proponents saw the Vietnam War as a fight just as noble as the fight against fascism that was won in the Second World War and certainly as important as Korea.

More complicatedly, there were men who opposed the war as ill-conceived or unwinnable, but did go to fight, because of their belief in the legitimacy of national action and out of their loyalty to the other Americans who were fighting. To shun the call, to these men, would have meant to abandon their brothers.

The Vietnam War has become such a symbol of a deep divide in American political life that it will probably not be honestly or accurately assessed during the lifetimes of those Americans who were alive during both the war itself and the domestic battle in its aftermath. For our purposes, it suffices to say that in terms of how military service is perceived today by whole swaths of our population, Vietnam changed everything. By the late 1970s the widespread perception—particularly among the educated classes—of the armed services was that it was full of the underclass, drug users, and people who couldn't make it anywhere else.

AFTER VIETNAM

The legacy of Vietnam still hangs over many opinion leaders' perceptions of the military. For instance, Terry Moran, the chief White House correspondent for ABC News, has been quoted as saying, "There is . . . a deep antimilitary bias in the media. One that begins from the premise that the military must be lying, and that American projection of power around the world must be wrong. I think that that is a hangover from Vietnam, and I think it's very dangerous."[20]

Congress responded to the disaster that the draft had become, with its many "deferments" that favored the well connected, the wealthy, the college students, and the lucky by creating the All-Volunteer Force. The services, the Army in particular, then began the slow process of rebuilding themselves. What a relief! No more protests! Without a hot war or a draft, activists lost interest in the military. (It is interesting to speculate about how widespread the antiwar protests would have been if there had been an all-volunteer military before the Vietnam War started.)

THE MILITARY ESTABLISHMENT'S ROLE IN THE CLASS MAKEUP OF THE ARMED SERVICES

Once established, the All-Volunteer Force was increasingly smaller and more specialized. Following the stinging experience of Vietnam, the military leadership was reconfiguring itself, repairing the damage it sustained in morale, discipline, and training. And perhaps the military establishment was just as happy not to have a noisy section of the society fighting the culture wars on its turf.

The smaller military emphasized highly skilled and motivated

---

20. Terry Moran, quoted in Nicholas Lemann, "Right Hook," *The New Yorker,* August 29, 2005, p. 36.

troops, deemphasizing the idea that broader representation was desirable. Increasingly, the military wanted professionals who took years to train. The services wanted to recoup their investment in these troops by retaining their members for longer periods. Increasingly, individuals signed up for five or six years at a stretch, depending on their field of specialty. The Department of Defense "reallocated" resources it had in ROTC programs at private universities, demonstrating that reaching out to that demographic was not a priority for the Pentagon. To help understand the military leadership's mind-set post-Vietnam and their desire to keep the All-Volunteer Force professional, rather than to regress to a citizen force, it is useful to contemplate again some of the range of American military interventions post-Vietnam that the government demanded.

* ZAIRE 1977–78: The Carter administration provided military aid and airlifted Moroccan troops to help President Mobutu quell uprisings.
* LIBYA 1981–89: Following many terrorist acts by Libya, two Libyan jets were shot down in Libyan airspace, and President Gadhafi's residences were bombed. Attempts were made to assassinate and overthrow Gadhafi, after he ordered the Pan Am 103 terrorist bombing.
* LEBANON 1982–84: U.S. Marines expelled the PLO and backed the Christian Phalangists. The Navy bombed and shelled Muslim and Syrian positions.
* HONDURAS 1983–89: U.S. troops were sent to establish bases near borders in order to stop the communist leaders in Nicaragua and support the counterinsurgency in El Salvador and Guatemala.
* GRENADA 1983–84: An invasion four years after a communist revolution in this island of 110,000 was launched to stop the island from becoming a Soviet satellite state.

* BOLIVIA 1986: The U.S. Army assists raids on the cocaine regions.
* PHILIPPINES 1987–1990s: Site of U.S. military bases. The CIA/Pentagon aided the government in a counter–Islamic terrorism campaign and provided air cover for the government.
* PANAMA 1989–90: The U.S. sent 27,000 troops to invade and overthrow the government of Manuel Noriega under the war on drugs.
* LIBERIA 1990: U.S. troops were sent to evacuate civilians during a civil war.
* SAUDI ARABIA 1990–91: U.S. troops, 540,000 of them, and jets countered Iraq's invasion of Kuwait. Forces also deployed in Oman, Qatar, Bahrain, UAE, and Israel.
* GULF WAR 1991: The UN-sanctioned Desert Storm operation, which included a naval blockade of Iraqi and Jordanian ports, bombings, and troops to expel Iraqi troops from Kuwait.
* IRAQ 1991–2003: The U.S. and British forces enforced no-fly zones over Iraq, based on U.N. Security Council Resolution 688. U.S. jets flew out of Saudi Arabia and Turkey and were fired on almost daily.
* YUGOSLAVIA 1992–94: The U.S. led a NATO naval blockade of Serbia and Montenegro (rump Yugoslavia).
* SOMALIA 1992–93: A UN-sanctioned humanitarian mission, Operation Restore Hope.
* BOSNIA 1993–95: No-fly zone patrolled in the civil/religious war, which erupted as the Bosnian Serbs went to war. The U.S./NATO bombed Bosnian-Serb positions, to force Serbs into the Dayton peace agreement.
* HAITI 1994–96: A naval blockade against a Haitian military government. Forced the government from power by threatening invasion of the country. Peacekeeping mission after generals stepped down from power.

⋆ BOSNIA 1995–2004: NATO peacekeeping operation to enforce Dayton Accords.

⋆ ZAIRE (CONGO) 1996–97: U.S. Marines sent to guard Rwandan Hutu refugee camps in area where Congo revolution began.

⋆ LIBERIA 1997: U.S. Troops sent to assist in evacuation of foreigners.

⋆ SUDAN 1998: Missile attack on a pharmaceutical plant alleged to be a nerve gas plant.

⋆ AFGHANISTAN 1998: Missile attack on Al Qaida training camps.

⋆ IRAQ 1998: Four days of intensive air strikes after UN weapons inspectors alleged Iraqi obstructions.

⋆ YUGOSLAVIA 1999: The U.S/NATO intervention.

⋆ KOSOVO 1999: NATO peacekeeping operation to enforce UN Resolution 1244, which terminated the Kosovo war.

⋆ MACEDONIA 2001: NATO troops employed to partially disarm Albanian terrorists.

⋆ AFGHANISTAN 2001: Bombings of Taliban and Al Qaida targets as a part of the War on Terror in response to 9/11 terrorist attacks. U.S. Army Special Forces and Northern Alliance overthrew the Taliban regime.

⋆ AFGHANISTAN 2001————: Multinational peacekeeping operation plus attempts to eradicate Al Qaida and Taliban.

⋆ IRAQ 2003: First implementation of President Bush's preemptive strike strategy to be a part of the War on Terror.

⋆ IRAQ 2003————: Initially the postwar occupation of Iraq. Subsequently evolved into the military support of, first, appointed and then elected Iraqi government in fighting the internal insurrection and terrorism.

⋆ HAITI 2004: U.S./French/Canadian intervention to prevent civil war.

The military leadership knew how often their civilian leaders were calling them into action in the past several decades. Even before 9/11, surveys of the state of the armed forces were drawing attention to the high operational tempo—troops were being used a great deal, perhaps even too much to be sustainable, in everything from "peacekeeping" missions to covert operations. And whatever they were saying about the world on American campuses, the military leadership understood that in the post–Cold War vacuum, their civilian leaders would be calling on them to keep order and sustain the open sea lanes that are the prerequisite to the prosperity their countrymen demand.

GOOD SHORT WARS

About the time that the class distinctions of military service had become thoroughly entrenched, we had a few popular, quick, spectacularly covered, low-casualty wars, most notably the Gulf War of 1991 and the bombing of Serbia in 1999. This began a new (post-Vietnam, that is) era of high regard for the military. Those clean-cut people in uniforms seemed like surprisingly good guys, and they fought short exciting conflicts. Moreover, Americans didn't get killed, or not many, and certainly no one you knew. The precision weapons developed to roll back the Soviet Army in a potential worldwide conflict could be brought to bear on tin-pot dictators and other assorted bad guys, whiz-bang gadgets that looked like next-generation video games. It was good to be in charge, sort of like rooting for American Olympic basketball teams in the good old days before other countries learned how to play well enough to beat us.

But the high regard was at arm's length. It did not involve many people running down to their recruiter's office. It just meant that when troops came back home, they got interviewed by sympathetic hosts on the morning talk shows and were not spit on by protesters. Although the public image of the military had undergone a virtual complete rehabilitation since Vietnam, this had not brought the upper class back to its ranks.

5. The Rights of the Individual Trump the Virtues of the Citizen

"We have the Bill of Rights. What we need is a Bill of Responsibilities."

—Bill Maher

A woman in a Beverly Hills restaurant who learned that Kathy's husband was in the Marines told Kathy that she would find it "worthwhile for my sons to go into the military to help stabilize Darfur." But since she could never trust the government to use her sons only for actions she thought were worthwhile, she would never be in favor of them serving. This seemed to us like a good example of a larger phenomenon: life understood in the sole context of personal choice and an individual's politics.

Americans have always been individualists. But this individualism, which became more robust in the 1960s, has since been reinforced by the postmodernist movement of the late 1970s and the 1980s. This movement argued that truth is relative, that those who win the power struggle get to define the truth, and that new or different "truths" can be equally valid to different people. What "I" decide is therefore not only subjective but also as "valid" as what a culture, country, or another individual may think. In the words Gertrude Stein used to describe Oakland, there is no "there, there" in this view. And there certainly is no national truth that overrides individual preference. In this context the call to national service is hard to make. There are no national let alone universal truths, just individual experiences. So the military has to be pitched as just one more personal choice.

Kathy

A friend of mine—a graduate student whose husband is in the Army Special Forces—wrote me a letter after she and I had been comparing how becoming military wives had changed us.

> There were times when I was first dating my husband, Mike, when our different worldviews got clear. In winter 2002, we were snowed in in my Chicago apartment. He couldn't return to Fort Meade (where he was supposed to be for some meetings), nor could I cross the twenty blocks to my office. But I had a laptop, and a report on teen STDs to write. I gazed out the window to the frozen Chicago River framed between high buildings, twirled my pencil, and announced, "I sure don't feel like writing this report."
>
> Mike looked up from the book he was reading and commented, "I don't see what that has to do with anything."
>
> I was, as my French mother would have said, *"bouche bée."* Up until that moment, I had in fact thought that "how I felt" was the most relevant piece of information that existed. I grew up during the pop-psychology movements of the '80s, where we all learned the right way to discuss things, as in, "that makes me feel . . ." In my mind, I had to get "inspired" to write the report, psyched up for it.

In Mike's world, in contrast, people don't say things like "and how does that make your feel?" No one asks a Special Forces soldier if he feels like doing a chemical weapons exposure drill, for instance. But it serves a purpose, so you do it.

I've learned the same thing in my exposure to the military. Something needs to be done, so you do it. This particularly resonates when you've got a husband at war. There are a lot of things you need to do when you might rather lie in bed—write your husband engaging e-mails about your day, help with picnics and functions on base that help the group get through the deployment, give your kids decent meals rather than fast food.

American culture has brought us to a place where feelings matter most, our personal choices and beliefs are sacrosanct, and those choices identify us as a consumer and exemplar of life's experiences. In this sort of world it is hard to understand military service. Military people don't—can't—make personal choice central. They don't choose their missions or even where they live.

It was the spring of 2003. We had gotten through the initial Iraq invasion; the regime of Saddam Hussein had fallen. I was relieved, but still feeling a bit stunned by the experience of having my husband in so much danger. I was visiting an old school classmate and trying to convey my amazement at what my husband had experienced in Iraq. She looked at me for a moment and then said, "He loves that shit."

I was speechless. My friend didn't have a framework for understanding what Greg was doing. He must be at war because he likes it—it must be some kind of macho or extreme sports–type predilection for thrills that would lead him to put himself in that position. So says the twenty-first-century American. Military men and women have choices—therefore they choose to walk into danger and discomfort.

This kind of packaging for bravery diminishes it, and makes it okay for other people not to do it. After all, liking that kind of "shit" is a little suspect, isn't it? It's a bit more civilized not to like it. In fact, though, the bravery of the soldier is not the bravery of the person "into" bungee jumping, proving to himself and the world that he's capable. Rather, service is a gift to other people—it's a gift to the country, to fellow soldiers, an attempt to use your training to fulfill a task that the country has asked you to do.

Would my husband rather have been taking the kids to the zoo? Yes, he would have preferred that to the Iraqi desert. In fact, most men and women at war would rather be someplace else. My husband went because he was trained, he was asked, and so he went to contribute what he could. Feelings were not the point.

Frank

In November of 1999, Genie and I flew to Savannah, then drove up to Parris Island to join John for "Family Day" before graduation. To see John in uniform was a shock. To sense that he was at home, in this strange place, and nervous at our presence was a surprise. How had we become unfamiliar to our son? To sense this new thing—represented by his uniform—that had come between us was unsettling. The fact that John was subject to rules that separated him from us, "We have six hours of liberty but can't leave Parris Island," made me feel queasy. It was as if John had somehow lost control over his own life. I felt as if I were visiting him in some kind of prison. I was completely unused to anyone in our family being part of something that he or she could not walk away from, or that superseded our family's ties.

John had written us boot camp letters that were confident about his achievements. But I still was trying to grasp what had happened to him, why did he seem so different? And how had our relationship changed?

Ever since he'd joined up, and especially after he graduated, I'd been asking myself: What will John "get" out of joining the Marine Corps? In the winter of 1999, in the context of the book we were writing together, I'd written to John asking how the Marines had changed him. John wrote an e-mail answer to me from his base in Fort Huachuca, Arizona (where he was being trained for his job in military intelligence). And with these lines came my first real inkling of the divide between the life of military service and the more selfish life that I had known.

> After we all got to Parris Island, our reasons for wanting to be Marines changed and deepened or we got sent home. By the end of boot camp each of us believed that we might be sent to different parts of the world to die in causes that might seem utterly ridiculous. . . . We were aware that we would be involved in actions in which we had no say whatsoever. We knew we would do the job and do it well, not because we wanted to kill people or die, but because each Marine relies on another Marine watching his or her back.
>
> That was the difference between the reasons most of us had for joining and the reality of what boot camp turned us into, and how it changed our thinking. For whatever half-assed reason we joined, by the time boot camp was done we were aware of our responsibility to the other Marines who depended on us. We were also aware of the tradition we were going to uphold. We were constantly reminded of it by the simple white markers all over PI, reminders of Marine battles and sacrifices for country and Corps, from the Boxer Rebellion to World War II, Korea, Vietnam, and Beirut.
>
> Most of all, loyalty to the Corps was something boot camp made tangible. By the end of boot camp we were trying to be good Marines out of loyalty to the Marine standing next to us and to those who would follow us onto the yellow footprints we

had stood on three long months ago. On Parris Island I came to see and believe what I was told; each mission is dependent on another that came before. When it came down to it, as any recruit could tell you by the end of his training, the Marine next to you is more important than you are.

Frank and Kathy

Postmodernism and cultural relativity allow statements to be true if you append the tagline "to me" onto them. Public service is important "to me." The soldier standing next to me is important "to me." Religion is a source of values "to me." Boot camp was of value "to me." To make broader claims—say, that military service is a good thing no matter how you feel about it—has fallen out of fashion.

Our "truths" have gotten smaller. They are not big truths that speak universally but small truths that are really nothing more than personal statements of subjective preference. Of course, when this method of seeing the world is placed in a certain context, its limits become obvious. For instance, even in the postmodern world this statement would draw some incredulous looks: "Killing Jews at Auschwitz seems bad to me." We assume that killing people in a concentration camp is bad period. But when it comes to the old assumptions about national service, even patriotism, these have passed from the realm of the given—true for everyone—to the realm of the personal, true "to me" or not true "to me."

The tolerance implicit in this kind of "to me" thinking and in the attendant theory of multiculturalism—something may be "true" or "good" for one culture but not for all cultures—is probably better than the alternative of jingoistic absolutism. But no social movement operates without unintended consequences. And the consequence of making things valid if they relate to the individual—the "me" in "to me"—is that the individual becomes the center of things, for better and worse.

As a result, individual choice and individual good becomes the basis of decision making. As historian Russell Weigley notes, Americans "stand for the liberation of the individual, in pursuit of a democratic society but also of economic gain and material gratification." All of which, Weigley goes on to say, stands in contrast to the purpose of military service.[1]

But in the modern era, individualism is central to self-consciously virtuous people too. Under the modern view, each person now is the best arbiter, through his or her individual conscience, of the greater good. Popular culture reinforces this idea in young people from their earliest Disney movie, where they are urged that "your duty is to your heart," "follow your dream," etc., to their adolescent years, where they hear "Luke, listen to your feelings!" and similar philosophies from popular entertainments day in and day out.

Under this construct, military duty is compelling only if you personally choose the cause at hand, or if it will in some way help your personal growth or your self-esteem. The idea of society choosing the cause, that you don't in fact even know what mission you might perform when you commit to serve, has become anathema to virtue since no virtue is possible without individual choice.

Today, it is easy for an observer to understand participation in military service as being simply about personal preference, something like a choice to take up bungee jumping—a bad idea for many, but okay for those sorts of people into that sort of thing. Otherwise military service is understood only as an expression of economic need, the best source of money for those who can't get more elsewhere. Or it is understood as a political choice, for people with a "hawkish" worldview, who thereby make a "personal statement" through joining.

---

1. Russell F. Weigley, "The American Civil-Military Cultural Gap: A Historical Perspective, Colonial Times to the Present," in Feaver & Kohn, eds., *Soldiers and Civilians,* p. 218.

At the same time that personal preference has come to reign supreme, the country has become more prosperous. Prosperity, for many people, has stimulated a reflex against things that are difficult, as if the goal of both childhood and adulthood is to avoid discomfort and risk. This development also works against the appeal of military service.

We see this point well illustrated in a nonmilitary context in *Coach: Lessons on the Game of Life,* by Michael Lewis. It is the story of Lewis's old private high school baseball coach and mentor in Florida, who ran afoul of a group of wealthy parents, offending them by being too strict with their teenage sons. The coach was legendary; generations of grateful graduates attributed their life's successes to the character development, the "life lessons," Lewis writes about.

The coach was about to be fired by a headmaster who believed that the parents were the "client" and as such they were entitled to anything they wanted. The coach's past students were raising money to build a new gym named for their mentor at exactly the same moment when the new crop of wealthy parents were holding meetings demanding he be fired.

Despite his outstanding track record, the coach was out of step with this generation's parent. For instance, the coach expected kids to show up for practice or not play. And he tended to think that there was only one way to run a team: his way. He demanded that during vacations the team members work on their fitness. He told one boy he was disappointed that the boy had not kept his promise to lose ten pounds over a vacation and had instead gained weight, thus making him unfit to play. "He called my son fat!" railed the furious father. In other words, the coach maintained standards. And these standards were not subjective. They were related to something measurable, the objective reality of winning. If his students wanted to feel good about themselves, they had to earn it. And if they wanted to win, there were certain things they had to do, regardless of their feelings about them.

Lewis described how past generations regarded their old coach.

One successful man after another—top athletes, top business leaders, good fathers, fulfilled and satisfied men in all walks of life—bore witness to the effect the coach's life lessons had on them. These were lessons such as team before self, that hard work, even suffering, produces results not attainable otherwise. It was the same sort of testimony that a million former soldiers, sailors, airmen, Coast Guardsmen, and Marines give about their drill instructors or a particular officer or noncommissioned officer—someone who demanded more than they thought they had in them, the sort of person who raises standards by personal example, leading from the front.

Child-development experts have consistently written about new parenting trends in the same terms as Lewis did. According to psychologist Wendy Mogel, parents of children in her wealthy West Los Angeles practice are increasingly working to keep their offspring "protected from any sort of danger, relieved of pressure to perform or take responsibility, and sufficiently stimulated by having lots of fun things to do."[2] To Mogel and many other expert commentators, this trend is terribly harmful for children. It leaves them emotionally incapable of facing the actual challenges of life—marriages when they hit a bad patch, jobs when things don't go their way, society when it asks something of them.

Sociologist Jim Burk describes this phenomenon as a natural outgrowth of a public culture in which the only agreed upon ethic is the utilitarian ethic, based on what John Stuart Mill called the "happiness principle." The popular version of utilitarianism misunderstands Mill, and, according to Burk, leads us "to prefer (and to think ourselves right to prefer) pleasure over pain, profit over loss, winning over losing—and to suppose nothing else matters more."[3]

---

2. Wendy Mogel, *The Blessing of the Skinned Knee* (New York: Penguin Books, 2001) p. 19.
3. James Burk, comments to the authors, September 12, 2005.

We recognize the same sort of overprotective parents described in *Coach* in an anti-military-recruitment group that has a Web site name so revealing it's funny: leavemychildalone.org. The sole purpose of the group is to stop military recruiters from ever asking their children to even consider serving their country. And since presumably these parents know that they are unlikely to thereby eliminate the military, the implication is that someone else's child should be asked to serve, just not "my child."

It seems to us that this is the ultimate expression of the postmodern "to me" idea of truth. And it also fits the profile of the new hyperindividualism. We find the position expressed by Leave My Child Alone untenable and shortsighted for our society.

Just imagine our society if and when this risk-averse and terminally selfish sentiment takes over. We need firemen to save people in the Twin Towers. Leave my child alone! We need teachers to work with underprivileged children in a dangerous part of town. Leave my child alone! We need National Guardsmen and active-duty soldiers to save drowning people stranded in their homes in New Orleans! Leave my child alone!

The group is sponsored by a consortium of progressive organizations and is a good example of people who consider themselves to be pro–public service, but take exception with the military. Leave My Child Alone declares itself not to be anti-military—they "support the troops" but want to protect their children from "aggressive recruiting tactics," citing "privacy concerns." They *do* want their children to be aggressively contacted by potential corporate employers or top colleges, maybe even the Peace Corps, but not by the military. Any contact at all apparently is too great an imposition.

The mind boggles at what the reaction to such a group would have been from most Americans in any other period of our nation's history, before the advent of postmodern thinking combined with hyperindividualism. We wonder how Harry Hopkins—Roosevelt's chief adviser, whose son volunteered and was killed in the Pacific fighting the Japanese—or Teddy Roosevelt—who resigned as assistant secretary of the navy to join the Rough Riders, then sent his own sons to serve in World War I—would have reacted.

The attitude Lewis's coach faced is now confronting the whole country—enfranchise me, give me the benefits of citizenship, but don't ask me to do anything that I don't feel like doing.

Here is a letter Frank got from the mother-in-law of a young embattled recruiter. It seems to us to sum up the collision of the old idea of duty with the postmodern culture of individualism:

> My son-in-law is a recruiter in Ohio, a sergeant at the ripe old age of twenty-one. He is finding recruiting to be a real challenge. Parents have been less than gracious when he contacts their children. Many have been rude and hateful. The prevailing attitude has been "let someone else do it" because my child shouldn't have to face difficulty or danger.
>
> Recruiters need civilian advocates. We could appeal to the parents on a different level than the soldier or Marine in uniform! I find it frustrating that most people in this country are completely unaffected by this war unless they have someone serving in the military. There is no sense of duty or sacrifice. I fear for this country.
>
> Beth Miller

POLITICS VERSUS CITIZENSHIP

Some people consider their reaction against military service to be a political statement or a statement about policy choices, not about comfort or safety. However, military service is not a referendum on political activity. "Should the country engage in this war?" is politics; "Shall I serve my country because it asks for its members to serve?" is patriotism. It is a gesture of profound citizenship to declare that "I will take part in this country and its collective decision making, because someone needs to do it." It is also an affirmation that there are bigger truths than simply what seems true (or fun) "to me."

One result of our relatively new, politicized vision of American life is that military action, and hence the meaning of military service, has become divided into our "good" wars or missions and our "bad" wars. The person of conscience might imagine themselves fighting in the Civil War or in World War II, but refusing to fight in the Spanish-American War or in Vietnam. Lost in this formulation is the fact that actual events are always far more complicated and controversial than in our easy history.[4]

Whether or not to use military action is an important issue. And it is crucial for society to engage in asking hard questions. But that questioning has to be done by civilians, not soldiers (who should consider the legality of their individual actions in war, but not "Is this the most successful policy?"). And some civilians have to be willing to relinquish the perquisites of a citizen for a space of time and become soldiers. This act ties the military action back to the citizenry and makes action legitimate. To abandon either the citizen's connection to the soldier or the soldier's traditional faithfulness is to undermine our nation's ability to act.

The government needs to provide both a rationale and transparency to people to keep support of any military action strong, or be

---

4. In *Stolen Valor,* authors B. G. Burkett and Glenna Whitley reveal how the received orthodoxies about the Vietnam War have led to a tremendous discounting of the contributions and success of those involved in that war (during the conflict, and later in society). They also document the ready acceptance of tragedies that didn't happen but were claimed by a significant number of people who asserted veteran status without ever having served in the war. There were tragedies in that war—but just as rapes by American service members in World War II are not spoken of, heroism and greatness in Vietnam are rarely acknowledged.

willing to change course. Yet if we do not maintain some individual humility, the country can't act as a country.

That is where the nation as a nation takes precedence and in some mysterious way is "wiser." It has a longer life than any individual. And the needs of that national life sometimes are different than the needs of the individual. The nation also "learns" at a different pace. And if the individual wants to contribute to his or her nation's longer life and collective wisdom—in other words, to the well-being of the place that individual's children and grandchildren will someday live in—the individual has to forgo his or her own version of "to me" truth from time to time. That is how nations, cultures, and communities survive. It is what we call civilization: "to me" becomes "to us." And this is what makes an orderly and decent life possible.

The true challenge for the individual American citizen is to enter into the long experiment in self-rule of our nation of 300 million souls and, in doing so, be willing to vest basic legitimacy in our democracy and its core institutions. Why should we? The government makes so many mistakes! Perhaps Winston Churchill provided the best answer—democracy is the worst form of government, except for all the alternatives.

Buying into democratic government *does* mean that we should take the long view and recognize the value of strong national institutions. The best way to prevent mistakes is to have more of the populace, not less, invested in the big decisions. The Not-With-My-Child attitude applied to the workings of democracy spells the end of the process by which we all survive.

No country can have a military unless people who serve do so for the sake of the country, rather than measuring each action taken by the government to see if they can approve of it or if it seems true "to me." "Do I agree with the national strategy?" or "Am I getting enough out of this?" are not the sort of questions that allow a military to be an arm of national action. These questions do not lend themselves to the continuity of democracy in any sphere: after all, we do not pay taxes only for programs we approve of or stop paying taxes when the "other candidate" wins the election. We do not stop obeying the rule of law because there are laws passed by Congress or rulings by the Supreme Court we may disagree with.

The illogic of tying military service to individual political tastes breaks down when you consider the sweep of world events. If military service is political, what happens when we change presidents? Do one set of soldiers quit and another set take over? What happens when a "good war"—say, invading Afghanistan—evolves into a "bad war"—say, Iraq, when there were no weapons of mass destruction? How about when a "good war" bogs down because of the failure to kill some future bin Laden? What happens when a "good president" we voted for inherits a "bad war"? If one day we suddenly want the military around very much, as virtually everyone did on September 12, 2001, and in the aftermath of Hurricane Katrina, where should the men and women of the military suddenly come from?

6. How the Gap Affects the Military and the Mission

You call us victims, thereby robbing us of any account-
ability and responsibility for our actions. You make it
sound as if we were conscripted to fight this battle.
— CH (CPT) Kevin Wainwright,
Chaplain 1-113th FA BN

The military is aware that there is much that it does not share with Americans who don't serve—both with those in the larger American culture and those in the country's economic and cultural leadership. The military's view of itself is positive, but we also detect a kind of embattled alienation, and perhaps even a creeping sense of superiority.

Like Spiderman, today's American soldier can feel that his (or her) position in life is to protect good citizens who suspect his motives and who may see him as a kind of caricature. Those in the military may feel there are parts of their military culture that are superior to the larger American culture, but that few outside their world understand them. The military may have the mission, but many of its members feel that the civilian world has the voice.

As it happens, some of those who wear uniforms never leave their personal enclave of close friends and neighbors, thus reinforcing their isolation. Many military people live exclusively in or near base communities steeped in the military world, with people who share beliefs about the basic premises of life. They may have a negative view of the dominant civilian culture, or they may rarely think about it at all, the way some upper-middle-class people never think about the military. A few in the military family occasionally cross the divide and experience culture shock, somewhat as both of us do as we straddle the disconnect and find it an unusual place to be.

The divide between military and civilian life is self-reinforcing. And it is becoming increasingly political. The majority of military personnel identify themselves as Republicans. And a disproportionate number of academics and those in the media identify themselves as Democrats.[1] In other words, our nation's defenders mostly vote one way and those who shape opinion (and educate our elites) mostly vote the other way, at a time when the political and cultural divisions in our country are deeper than ever.

Let's say a cultural gap exists and that many members of the military feel superior to or at least alienated from civilian culture. So what? After all, probably other professional groups have felt this exceptionalism—doctors, for instance. Some professional groups may even feel they are underappreciated by civilian culture (two that Kathy belongs to, lawyers and those in politics and government, leap to mind!). But few in the upper middle class oppose their children's joining the bar or seeking public office. Moreover, the military has a special role in society. Bluntly put—they have the guns.

---

1. Holsti, "Of Chasms and Convergences," in Feaver and Kohn, *Soldiers & Civilians,* 28, table 1.3.

No one in America expects a military coup. Thankfully, in our society that idea is laughable. But the military is an arm of U.S. power abroad. The military will be needed regardless of who sits in the White House and what political party is in power. And in a crisis, all Americans depend on the military. Its health can only be undermined by a sense of alienation.

Kathy

"Sophie!" I yell. "We're not on base—you can't play there." My seven-year-old is learning that the larger society has different rules, it's a different kind of place, and I wonder what effect that has on her. We live on a small air station in North Carolina, and in many ways it's like living in 1960. My second-grader and preschooler can pack a picnic and ride their bikes to the playground for an hour or two without me hovering over them. Early-elementary-school kids here can walk to school by themselves, read books in the children's section of the Military Exchange (PX), while Mom shops at a different part of the store. And yes, that seems better to me than the lockdown most American neighborhoods seem to experience.

Unlike 1960, the issue of race here is unremarkable. To children on base, men and women of a different color are not the "other," but one of us. They are Marines. That most potentially scary creature of all to most adult women, a strange nineteen-year-old man, is not threatening on base, even if encountered at night, on a walk. Paradoxically, even when Sophie's father was away fighting a war, there was probably less fear in her daily life, more confidence in her surroundings, than for her friends in places she used to live, in San Diego and Washington, D.C.

Those strange nineteen-year-old men, in fact, are people I know I can count on as a mother. There have been several occasions when I've arrived at the local airport, tired children in tow, one of them sleeping, four suitcases to lug plus a stroller. In the Jacksonville,

North Carolina airport I know I can go up to any group of Marines and ask for their help. More than once, I've had one standing outside by the car watching my sleeping three-year-old while I checked in, then waiting with my luggage while I parked the car. These young men don't know I'm a Marine wife. But I've asked for their help, and invariably received it. Changing planes, I can trust someone with a high-and-tight haircut to carry my sleeping forty-pounder—it's a different kind of sense of responsibility to others.

Out in my old communities, there is a carefully calibrated sense of avoiding imposition on each other's busy families. "Playdates" need to be scheduled well in advance (if at all). Here on base I know I can count on my neighbors in a pinch, even if they are folks I've never formally socialized with. And I, in turn, would rearrange my schedule for them—to watch their children, drive them to pick up a fixed car, and so on. When upper-middle-class women complain about the sense they have of being alone and without support in books such as *Perfect Madness,* I can't help feeling that we humble Marine families seem to have figured out something that they haven't, or that we have something they believe is available only in countries like France or Sweden (where it is not one's community, but the state, that solves their problems for them).

It's easy for me to look at a lot of modern culture and find parts of military culture more appealing. The evidence is detailed not only in *Perfect Madness,* but also in books such as *Bowling Alone,* which speaks of the alienation individuals feel from each other, or *The Cheating Culture,* which argues that a pattern of widespread cheating is unraveling American culture in business and the professions. *Is the American Dream Killing You?* explores how "the market" has re-placed meaning in American society—this is not a problem that plagues the military. These analyses all paint unattractive pictures of a larger culture that contrasts with the culture I live in. I know, since I'm connected to the civilian world and love that world too, that there's more to the overall picture than that. But what if you don't have those connections? If you have grown up in the military, marry in it, and remain there, what does the larger culture look like? This is not an abstract question, since a great number of military families, an increasing number, are following a family tradition of service.

I heard Sophie and her friend Summer talking one day, and Summer declared that when she grew up she planned to marry a Marine. That pricked up my ears, but what really got my attention was when Sophie volunteered that Summer could marry my son, Charley.

"Oh," I said. "Is Charley going to be a Marine?"

"Well, I *hope* so," Sophie answered.

Military exceptionalism—the sense that there is something better about military society than larger society—used to bother me. Sometimes I would feel that people connected to the armed forces thought they were the only ones serving their country or living patriotic lives. What about police officers, teachers, firemen, volunteers for AmeriCorps? Politicians and bankers do something vital for the country too. And it would bother me to hear military families talk about how much safer they felt on base. Now I wonder if my son and daughter will come to share those feelings. It is hard to tell stories about Daddy being a hero without conveying a bit of a slight to those daddies who don't take such dramatic risks on behalf of our country.

Frank

I have gained a rather backhanded insight into how the military community feels about the civilian world. Military and former military personnel will compliment me on "not being like most civilians." I am even invited to events to which I have no right to go, like the November 10 Marine Corps birthday ball, celebrating the founding of the Marine Corps in 1775. And sometimes I am asked to speak, much as a new convert shares his or her testimony in a church.

What I didn't know when I started to write on the subject of my family's "conversion" into the military family—albeit a forced conversion—was that though there were tons of books on military history, many memoirs by military and former military people, and some recent scholarly works on various aspects of the military, there were not many contemporary writers who had *not* been in the military who were writing about their respect for the present-day military in personal terms.

In letters I got I couldn't help noticing a real *we*-against-*them* edge to a lot of the responses. And it wasn't just that "they" didn't understand "us." A negative view of the civilian culture exploded through many letters, even letters on other subjects. For instance, in the midst of an e-mail about military procurement, Dean Spraggins, a retired Air Force lieutenant colonel and Air Force Academy grad, class of 1975, wrote:

> Problems in procurement today are not trivial, but they are only exacerbated by the propensity of Congress to micromanage and meddle, by media and academia seething with overt, relentless hostility, by political correctness, and by an irresistible tendency to treat the military as no more than a playpen for social engineering experiments.[2]

I got the same sort of letters from readers who read an opinion piece I wrote for the *Washington Post* on the fact that when a soldier was killed, his family got only $12,000 in death-benefit compensation. (I'd compared what the civilian victims of 9/11 had received, an average of $3.5 million per family, to what the military families

---

2. Dean Spraggins, e-mail message to coauthor Frank Schaeffer, December 28, 2004.

received, $12,000. The law has since been changed and made more generous.) The article, reprinted in some thirty newspapers, generated a big response, most of which was from vets telling me that of course it was this way, the civilians and legislators never thought about them unless they needed the military. The recurring theme was that civilians—including the members of Congress and the president—don't care.

This feeling of alienation reminds me of another big change in my life that had occurred some years before my entry into the military family. In 1990, I converted to the Greek Orthodox Church. The fact that my late father had been a well-known Protestant theologian made for some interesting reactions. Many Greek Americans are within a generation or two of having suffered from discrimination. I met plenty of Greeks who had heard parents' and grandparents' horror stories about harassment and bigotry.

In both cases—"joining" the military family and joining the Orthodox Church—I had the experience of being an outsider welcomed as a new insider. In the case of the military "church" I "joined," this was reinforced during my several visits to the Parris Island Marine Corps Training Depot. The incredibly hardworking and ascetically dedicated Marine drill instructors spoke to me about the "nasty civilian" world they are saving the youth of America from, in much the same tones of missionary zeal I had often heard from Greek Orthodox monks during a visit to the monasteries of Mount Athos. "The world" is the problem to both monks and DIs.

Every DI sends his or her new "converts" out after graduation with a warning not to backslide into old bad civilian habits. The fact that the military sees its secondary role as that of "turning around lives" and "saving youth" is instructive. You don't save people from something you think is good.

When sleepy, often terrified recruits arrive on Parris Island, it is the middle of the night. This is what they first hear as they step from the bus onto the fabled yellow footprints that are painted on the street. A DI bellows:

"You are now aboard Marine Corps Recruit Depot Parris Island, South Carolina, and you have just taken a first step toward becoming a member of the world's finest fighting force, the United States Marine Corps. . . . The Marine Corps' success depends on teamwork—you will live, eat, sleep, and train as a team. The word 'I' will no longer be a part of your vocabulary. Do you understand?"

"Sir, yes sir!"

"Tens of thousands of Marines began outstanding service to our country on the very footprints where you are standing. Are you ready to carry forward their tradition?"

"Sir, yes sir!"

"Follow me!"

Follow me! Words Christ spoke to Saint Peter. Follow from where to where? From the old world, the old life into the new better life. The old life is put away and the new life undertaken with the understanding that the old life was inferior.

One hot morning during the summer of 2004, I had the honor to be standing near the parade deck of Third Battalion on Parris Island. (I was doing research for my novel *Baby Jack*.) Hundreds of cheering recruits surged onto the far end of the parade deck. They sprinted—a torrent of recruits in olive green T-shirts against the gray sky. They gathered in a throng on the wet pavement around Colonel Kelley, the base commander, and then sat down. He was about to address them. At the end of the "transformation," as the military refers to the intense life-altering change that takes place in boot camp, new soldiers, sailors, airmen, Coast Guardsmen, and Marines hear a speech like the one below, or something very like it, from an officer bidding him or her well-done and farewell. With a word change here or there it could be a sermon by a preacher to new converts.

Colonel Kelley—a tall, thin middle-aged man with close-cropped gray hair—stood in the middle of the circle turning from this side to that as he delivered his remarks. He was in running shorts and a sweat-soaked T-shirt—he had led the motivation run, the final exercise just before graduation.

"Within days, you young men and women will be in your specialty schools, then many will be sent into combat in Afghanistan and Iraq. Some here today will not be coming home. You are U.S. Marines: whether you are in uniform or in civilian gear, they ought to be able to tell that you are Marine by the way you hold yourself. Only those who are unconfident of their abilities think they need to act tough. We hold doors open for others. This is the responsibility you have earned. From now on it won't be somebody else's responsibility; it will be yours to uphold our tradition."

The faces of the recruits were rapt—no one moved.

"There are future Medal of Honor winners sitting to your right and to your left. We don't get the big paychecks, but we play for keeps. There is only one person who can diminish the respect for the Marine Corps, that's you. If you lower your standards, everyone will notice. You do not want to become like them: ordinary. Look into the eyes of your loved ones today after you graduate, and I guarantee that all you will see is love and respect the size of the Goodyear blimp."

"OORAH!" roared the recruits.

Kathy and Frank

Samuel Huntington, in his classic study, *The Soldier and the State,* said the armed services have "the outlook of an estranged minority."

More ominously, retired admiral Stanley Arthur has suggested that, "The armed forces are no longer representative of the people they serve. More and more, enlisted as well as officers are beginning to feel that they are special, better than the society they serve."

Thomas Ricks echoes this concern in his 1997 book, *Making the Corps,* asserting that "U.S. military personnel of all ranks are feeling increasingly alienated from their own country, and are becoming more conservative and more politically active than ever before."

Do officers and enlisted personnel believe their civilian leaders have their best interests at heart? A recent poll says, no, they do not.[3] At the same time, this poll found that armed service members think they as a group have higher moral standards than the nation they serve.[4]

An attempt to test this "cultural gap" using more scientific polling methods found that we are not at a crisis point yet. But both sides on the civil-military gap suspect that the other doesn't truly hold them in esteem. Researchers at Duke University conclude from their study that "civilians are confident that civilians respect the military, the elite military is confident that the military respects civilian society; each group, however, doubts to some degree whether the respect is reciprocated."[5]

On the other hand, in another study, a not-insignificant minority of 26 percent of enlisted service members disagreed with the statement that "most members of the armed forces have a great deal of respect for American civilian society."

The study found that senior military officers view civilian society far more negatively than do civilians in leadership positions.

---

3. *Military City* poll.
4. Gordon Trowbridge, "Today's Military: Right, Republican, and Principled," *Marine Corps Times,* January 5, 2004. Two-thirds in the *Military City* poll agreed with this position.
5. *Soldiers and Civilians,* Feaver & Kohn, eds. p. 143.

Moreover, few of the elite military officers agreed with *any* of the positive poll statements about civilian society.[6] Moreover, the more personal contacts an individual had with the military, the more likely the respondents were to hold views that civilian society is in moral crisis and that the military can help remedy the situation. Two-thirds of the elite military officers believe that political leaders are somewhat or very ignorant of military affairs.[7]

In other words, the alienation is real. How does it manifest itself in specific instances?

THE POLITICIZATION OF THE MILITARY

Kathy's next-door neighbor Jane was talking to Kathy in the front of their houses, where the lawns meet. Jane is a Marine wife, a former Marine herself, and a freelance writer. She had seen a commentary of Kathy's in *USA Today* that mentioned Kathy had worked in the Clinton White House. "I don't mean this in a mean way," Jane said, smiling. "But I've never actually met someone who considers themselves a Democrat. How did you decide that?"

Jane had never met a Democrat! That is a problem, and not just for Democrats trying to figure out why they keep losing elections. The ideal of our military, as we discussed before, is to be a nonpolitical entity. Today one can, and many do, post signs supporting (invariably Republican) candidates on the front lawn of their government military housing. That would have been unheard

---

6. TISS, p. 149. The questions at issue are: Q8a: The decline of traditional values is contributing to the breakdown of our society. Q8b: Through leading by example, the military could help American society become more moral. Q8c: The world is changing and we should adjust our view of what is moral and immoral behavior to fit these changes. Q8d: Civilian society would be better off if it adopted more of the military's values and customs.
7. TISS, p. 151.

of in previous generations. To a civilian, the idea that you shouldn't post a sign may sound like censorship—but military rules are different from civilian rules. A government house is government property.

As we write, the country as a whole is more Republican than it used to be. It happens, however, that there's a disproportionately high percentage of Democrats among those who rank in the professional, academic, and cultural leadership.[8] In contrast, there are a disproportionate number of Republicans in the military. Whatever the reason, the result is another factor in the widening divide between our civilian opinion-shaping elites and our military, who bear the brunt of public policy and complaints about that policy.

The political polarization between the so-called red and blue states has spilled over and helps reinforce the upper-middle-class sense that those who serve are the "other." And from the military point of view, the fact that most officers define themselves as Republicans means that they see the nonserving opinion-making classes as alien politically. Of course, as we have said, upper-class Republicans are little more likely to serve these days than privileged Democrats. But here we are talking about *perceptions*. And we believe that the perception that one political party is more sympathetic to the military is unhealthy for our democracy. We are not trying to ascribe blame, merely noting a perception that shapes attitudes that will impact our country.

In 1976, most of the military identified themselves as Independent, while 33 percent identified as Republican (still a larger proportion than the general public). But the members of the armed services have since abandoned this neutrality. Now 56 percent consider themselves Republican, and only 15 percent consider themselves

---

8. TISS, Table 1.3. Reported in Holsti, "Of Chasms and Convergences," in Feaver and Kohn, *Soldiers and Civilians*, p. 28.

Independent.[9] Partly, the preference for Republican over Democrat results from the actions or perceived actions of the parties. The military felt betrayed by the Democrats in Vietnam. Democratic presidents in fact sent the military into Vietnam in the first place. But the protesters who spit on our troops when they returned home were not Republicans. They may not have been Democrats either—and certainly those protesters horrified many Democrats—but as liberals or left-wingers they were associated with the Democratic Party. And to its detriment the Democratic Party did not do enough to separate itself from its most radical supporters. So however most Democrats actually felt about the military and even though tens of thousands of Democrats sent their children to serve, the perception remains that Democrats are the party of anti-military protest.

At the same time, the Republican Party reached out to and courted the military. Perhaps more important, the evangelical Christians created an alliance between themselves, the Republican Party, and the military beginning in the 1970s—something that's been well documented by political scientist Andrew Bacevich. This strategy has borne fruit in the current era, where the ties between these three groups—weak a generation ago—are now very strong.

This issue is one of perception, but in politics perception is reality. Here are the two gut-check questions: Who are critics of the military more likely to vote for? Who do the American people think is the party of Michael Moore? The fact that a rural or inner-city, Democrat-voting, working-class person is far more likely to actually serve than a wealthy Republican living in a big city is not the point. Regardless of whether or not it is fair that current Democrats are

---

9. The 1976 figures are from data in the Foreign Policy Leadership Project conducted by Professor Ole Holsti. The second set is from the 2005 *Military City* poll (13 percent identify as Democrats). Although the numbers are not from the same study or derived using the same techniques, they are a good indicator of the trend. The last year of the Holsti study was 1996. In that year, about 67 percent of military identified as Republican.

perceived as being, as one researcher put it, "viscerally antimilitary," that perception surely plays a role in the military person's choice of affiliation.[10] It may also play a role in which political party most Americans trust with national security issues.

But even if the Democrats are perceived—perhaps temporarily—as out of step with the military, why would the military abandon a tradition of public neutrality? One reason may have to do with the disconnect. In previous generations, as the domain of all classes, the military was also the domain of both parties. There was a general understanding that all members of society knew why the military was there and agreed with the need to have both a strong defense and the resolve to use it. But as the military's belief that the larger society understands and values the military has decreased, so the military's need to advocate on their own behalf has grown. This puts the military in the position of becoming just one more special-interest group lobbying a bitterly divided Washington for attention. And this is a function and unintended by-product of the "all-volunteer" military and the fact that one class of Americans has been absent.

The only credible way to alter perception and begin to depo-liticize the military is for Democrats, liberals, and others to begin to publicly, consistently, and loudly advocate for broad participation of their own in military service. If they do not, they can hardly complain that the military is alienated from their values and politics. And if Democrats do not follow words with action—in other words not just talk about it but actually serve and encourage their children to serve—the trend of the military representing one political party will harden into a fact. And that fact will change the American landscape in what seems to us to be a very dangerous way.

---

10. Densch, "Explaining the Gap," in Feaver and Kohn, *Soldiers and Civilians*, p. 323.

AT RISK AT HOME

As we noted in an early chapter, tension between the media and the military is a subject that has received some attention. It seems the feelings (or perceptions) go both ways. "Hostility of the military to the media is one of the dominant themes" of their findings, say the authors of a major study of civil-military affairs.[11] We have seen evidence firsthand of that perceived bias. For instance, in a letter to the editor of *USA Today* published in response to Kathy's essay about why elite youth should consider serving in the military, reader Art Schefler, a retired Air Force major from Shreveport, Louisiana, wrote, "I was shocked to read Kathryn Roth-Douquet's commentary. . . . Only very infrequently do I come across such praise for those who serve in the military."[12] And a letter Frank got from a military chaplain illustrates in more detail the aggrieved reaction many in the military have to the way the media portray them.

> April 24, 2004
> Greetings from Iraq,
>
> We have been watching the news, and it appears back at home that nothing is going right. Columnists like Andy Rooney write disparaging articles about us, and it can be quite demoralizing at times. Here is some of what he wrote followed by my response.
>
> OUR SOLDIERS IN IRAQ AREN'T HEROES
> By Andy Rooney April 12, 2004

---

11. TISS, p. 94. Note that a companion TISS study shows that "the press in fact treat the military quite favorably, but in a somewhat less laudatory manner than professional military publications." (Weigand and Palentz, 2001, as quoted in *Soldiers and Civilians*, p. 95).
12. Art Schefler, letter to the editor ("Commentary Gives Military Proper, Long Overdue Salute"), *USA Today*, January 20, 2005, p. 14A.

It would be interesting to have . . . our soldiers in Iraq to answer five questions. . . .

1. Do you think your country did the right thing sending you into Iraq?
2. . . . [H]ave we failed so badly that we should pack up and get out before more of you are killed?
3. . . . [D]o you think our highest command is out of touch with the reality of your situation?
4. If you could have a medal or a trip home, which would you take?
5. Are you encouraged by all the talk back home about how brave you are. . . ?

. . . We pin medals on their chests to keep them going. We speak of them as if they volunteered to risk their lives to save ours, but there isn't much voluntary about what most of them have done . . . many young people, desperate for some income, enlisted . . . in the National Guard or the Army Reserve to pick up some extra money and never thought they'd be called on to fight. . . . Most are victims, not heroes. . . .

This is my response:

Dear Mr. Rooney,

I can only assume that you do not think me or any other soldier serving in Iraq, especially guardsmen, as real, professional, military men and women. This is unfortunate for us. You have come to think of our nation's military as nothing more than a corps that our politicians have purchased through economic manipulation and educational incentives.

You call us victims, thereby robbing us of any accountability and responsibility for our actions. You make it sound as if we were conscripted to fight this battle.

I believe your intention is noble when you say we are victims, for victims must be rescued from the big and bad enemy called the state.

It has been the practice of late to parade on the news scene after scene of disgruntled military personnel and their families. This is fine, because they do exist. What we are missing is the other side of the story. You fail to present the single mother who has left her son in the care of her mother so that she can be over here. She misses her boy, and she is missing her chance to start college this year, but she would not think about abandoning her post as a medic because she is a professional.

I will respond to your five questions.

1. What I think about my civilian chain of command's decision to send me to Iraq does not make any difference. The military remains one of the few places where one cannot opt out of one's commitment when the terms of fulfillment become difficult. I do not remember in my oath that I said that I will protect and defend the Constitution when I feel like it.

2. I believe that we cannot make anyone be anything. I do believe that we can aid a nation in setting up the conditions for democracy to take root.

3. When has the highest command ever been in touch with the reality of my situation? This question is just plain silly.

4. I would worry about any soldier who said that he would prefer a medal to a trip home to his family. In fact, I would be tempted to take his weapon away from him. I doubt that a single Medal of Honor recipient woke up the morning of the event and said that it was his goal to win a medal that day. What we do want to do as soldiers is to perform with courage and resolve, not because we want medals, but because we do not want to let our buddies down.

5. Am I encouraged when a fifth-grade class writes telling our soldiers that they are thankful for our service and how proud of us they are? Am I encouraged when our employers assure us reservists that we will have our jobs waiting for us when we return home? Why, yes, I am.

As far as the motivations for service, you seem fairly eager to make a generalization that all of us in the National Guard only joined up because of the money and never thought we would go to war. What of the young person who signed up for the service out of a desire to serve her nation and give something back to the country that had given her so much? There is the appeal that the military might actually make us less selfish, more mature, and better people. What of the desire for camaraderie and equality?

Your article sparked a lively debate among my fellow soldiers, and we unanimously concluded that we were glad to live in a country where you are free

to express your opinion, no matter how misguided it might be. It is my hope that your news organization will have the courage to come out to visit us and hear our story. We are proud to serve our country, we miss our families, and we cannot wait to return home. We have our tough days and our proud days, but most of all, we are thankful that we have each other. We are thankful that, when we look into each other's faces, be they black or white, male or female, Christian, Jew, or Muslim, that we have each other. We do not want to serve with heroes, we want to serve with real people who are proud of who we are and where we come from.
Grace, Mercy, and Peace,
CH (CPT) Kevin Wainwright
Chaplain 1-113th FA BN

Again, we are not arguing that there are no tributes to the military in the media. But we have seen the perception among many in the military that the mainstream media and the elite media in particular do not understand them or cover them fairly.

HOW THE MILITARY COMPARES ITSELF TO OTHERS

Adding to the military's sense of alienation is their perspective that critics are quick to attack military shortcomings but don't put those problems in the context of American society at large. In fact, looking at the exact same issues, where civilians see shortcomings, military people see their culture as superior.

We have known JAG corps members (the military's lawyers) to be frustrated by the fact that while the scandals of Abu Ghraib were uncovered by the military investigators and prosecutors, many Americans believe that civilian newspapers exposed the wrongdoing. In reality, the majority of media "exposures" of real or alleged military bad behavior rely almost exclusively on internal military investigative reports or military whistleblowers who have gone to the media. In other words, the military or individual soldiers had discovered and set about reporting bad behavior or prosecuting *before* the public came to know of the issues. The same is true for the alleged Koran mishandling cases in Guantanamo Bay. But the reporters and editors rarely note the JAG officers' or its investigators' aggressive policing. Moreover, the military prison scandals failed to lead to any serious consideration of the conditions in our own civilian prison system in America.

The military has been more open, transparent, and diligent in investigating and punishing acts of sexual harassment than any top college has—most of which do not even keep statistics on the issue. If, for example, a female in uniform reports that her colleague of the same rank touched her face when she didn't want him to, a full investigation will be launched and the incident may be included in the service's statistics on sexual assault—because it involved un-wanted touching. No college or office place in America would count such incidents in considering its track records in male and female relations.

The widespread sexual-abuse scandal at the Air Force Academy got the attention it deserved. Heads rolled when it was found that not enough was done to foster a climate of respect for women cadets. Air Force brass lost pay, jobs, and pensions, as they should have. We know of no colleges where the presidents have lost their jobs because of sexual abuse on campus—even between faculty and students or between students, although evidence of such abuse surfaces in the press with depressing regularity.

And in contrast to our schools' decision to be hands-off with their students in terms of binge drinking, DUIs, cheating, or sexual promiscuity, the military still makes value judgments that it deems are to their soldiers' lasting benefit. For instance, it enforces counseling, and if need be, reprimands and disciplines, even sentencing soldiers to time in the brig for destructive or bad personal behavior while off duty. Take the example of both the Super Bowl and World Series wins in Boston between the years of 2001 and 2004, when students overturned cars and set them on fire. Had that happened with cadets following, say, the Army-Navy game, the police would not have had to ask a base commander to "do something" about it. Yet the big colleges in the Boston area refused to expel anyone after hundreds of "elite" students trashed whole neighborhoods. Nor do colleges (or prep schools) prosecute the healthy proportion of their populations that use, manufacture, or sell drugs. Drug use will put a member of the military behind bars, then out of uniform—one strike, you're out.

The military sees itself as ahead of the curve on social justice and equality too. The military certainly has as good a record of behavior, or better, on race and gender than most other institutions in our country, including our media, entertainment, corporate, and academic institutions.

Specifically, the U.S. military had African American officers, even generals, decades before the *New York Times* appointed even one African American as an editor. There are far more black and Hispanic military people in positions of command than there are at comparable levels in corporate America, for all the talk about affirmative action and all its endless rounds of self-conscious "sensitivity training."

As Charles Moskos and John Sibley Butler observed in their landmark study of race and the Army, the military is the only place in America where African Americans routinely boss whites around.[13]

---

13. Charles C. Moskos and John Sibley Butler, *All That We Can Be: Black Leadership and Racial Integration the Army Way* (New York: Basic Books, 1996).

And any visit to any Marine Corps, Navy, Army, Coast Guard, or Air Force graduation ceremony will put the visitor in a far more economically and racially diverse group than would a visit to virtually any other American institution.

The military is also more egalitarian than corporate, media, or academic America. The top general in the military makes eleven times in pay what the lowest ranking private earns. Contrast this to what the business leader in charge of Harvard University's $25-billion endowment makes—about $3 million a year—while the janitors earn salaries modestly above the minimum wage. Or to a corporation, where the CEO, even at a progressive company like Ben and Jerry's ice cream, makes hundreds of times what his lowest paid staff member makes, without anyone raising an eyebrow.

And contrast the health plan of Wal-Mart workers to that of privates in the Army. The lowliest recruit has the same health-care benefits as a general. At Wal-Mart, the janitors are hired from outside companies that employ part-time workers, often with no health care at all, while the owners and top executives enjoy lavish benefits.

The military understands itself to be a meritocracy in comparison to larger society. You don't need to "know somebody" to advance. Just do your job very well, and the military will consider you for promotion.

Finally, as every drill instructor will tell you, the civilians sent to boot camp these days leave much to be desired. Many arrive having no idea how to work in a team, how to shoulder responsibility, or how to put other people first. And the shortcomings of civilian life are showing up in new and disturbing ways. The military must spend more and more time on a higher and higher proportion of recruits trying to get them in the minimum physical and mental condition to even begin actual boot camp training. When it comes to basic physical fitness, fewer young men and women who volunteer

each year can do what most young volunteers could do just a generation ago. As one Army Ranger sergeant told Frank, "Parents are always telling me they worry about their kid being killed in a war. But
there are going to be a lot more American twenty-year-olds dying of
diabetes than get killed in Iraq. When I see the shape these kids arrive in [at boot camp], I want to tell parents the safest place for your
kid is in my platoon!"

The class differences, pay differences, failures of parents and
educators, and lack of standards and accountability in the civilian
world are not lost on military people. And, to put it mildly, members
of the military find it annoying to be criticized by a civilian world
that can't keep its own house in order.

A FOOT IN BOTH WORLDS

In the spring of 2005, we spoke to a small group of people with
one foot on each side of the civilian-military divide. We conducted
interviews with the current Harvard Law School students who
were in the military, recently served, or who would be going back
into the military upon graduation. They were eager to talk, almost relieved that anyone was paying attention to their service in
the context of their Harvard Law experience. They believed that
what they did in the way of service was vital, but misunderstood
by their Ivy League peers. They all agreed that the gap is real,
and a problem.

These students agreed on a number of things—that widespread
ignorance among elites about the military exists and threatens to
harm our country's policy-making ability, and that the emerging
elites are missing out on lessons of leadership and self-sacrifice that
one learns almost exclusively in the military these days. We found it
worthwhile to quote some of the thoughtful and articulate responses
that were submitted to us in writing:

... The disconnect is a problem because it breeds ignorance and creates an aristocracy. A misunderstood military
may be ostracized from mainstream society or, worse yet, im-
properly used for political purposes. Already, this may be happening. It is easy to throw stones at organizations one doesn't
understand. The military has become a target for many through
its disciplined performance of orders from its civilian leaders
(i.e., the "torture" memos and handling of detainees, as well as
the "don't ask, don't tell" policy).

When it is not "my child" serving, we make decisions from
a detached, often uninformed, point of view. My argument derives from experience. Before joining the military, although
I would pray for those soldiers who were in Desert Storm, I
never experienced an attachment to the war effort or had an
understanding of the hardships involved with uprooting thousands of families to deploy overseas. I never questioned the
decisions made by our civilian leaders or worried about the suffering that others would endure. However, during my deployment to Iraq, I saw the true atrocities of war and the secondary
and tertiary effects it would have on families and individual
soldiers. Making decisions that affect others' lives has serious
ramifications. Knowing the implications involved is essential to
making informed and effective decisions. This is an endemic
problem that has serious ramifications. Rushing into conflicts
by sending "their children" and quickly withdrawing after
realizing it is "our children" tarnishes the reputation of the
United States.

My experience with the military has been exceptionally
educational. I came from a family with only one member with
a military background and no combat experience. I matricu-
lated at West Point because of the educational opportunities
available. Without serious thought to a military career, I aspired

to join the medical corps and perceived the military medical profession to be similar if not identical to what I would experience in the private sector.

However, after two years at the Academy, I learned that military personnel did not solely enforce policy through force. In addition, military personnel acted as the ambassadors to the world through stability and support operations abroad, leadership of America's sons and daughters at home, setting the example of leadership for civilian executives, and were the pinnacle of ethics for the country.

Ivy League students are ignorant about the military. Like others in society, the Ivy League gains most of its knowledge from the media and few have experiences with a close friend or family member who has served in the military. Many times I have heard, "You are the first person I have ever met who was in Iraq. How is it over there?"

. . . We all make judgments based on the limited information we receive. However, the judgments made from Ivy League students and faculty are often more vocal than others and thus can be more damaging. At one such Ivy League school several panels have discussed military activity without a subject-matter expert on the military (no military representative or former military member). While discussing the most pressing issues of today is admirable, the dearth of military knowledge often skews the debate. . . .

I have had several troop-leading experiences in my five years in the Army. The vast majority of the soldiers I served were very bright, hardworking, and patriotic. Most joined the military to earn money for college or as a stepping-stone to a greater career. After serving their initial enlistments, however, most of these soldiers decided to remain in the military and serve their country in a very honorable way. The military often does that. While seemingly tough and stoic on the outside, most find the military to be endearing and exciting. The military is a large family, one very different from society as a whole because of its common bond and commitment to service and sacrifice for the nation's good.

Kevin J. Terrazas

I do think there is a disconnect between privilege and the military. I grew up privileged in the sense that I had a lot of options as a child, though I was solidly middle class: my father was an Army officer and my mother was a high school teacher.

From the top public high schools, to Rice University, to Stanford graduate school, to Harvard Law School, it has always been rare to see someone with a military parent, or who has been in the military, or who is planning on joining. So there's a physical disconnect between both groups, and I've spent years of my life on both sides of the line.

I think there are problems with the disconnect. To me, the military/privilege divide feels like the red/blue divide in America. I think that if you look at maps of recruiting and maps of the recent presidential elections, you'd see a lot of correlation.

My feeling is that the military and our nation both benefit when children of privilege serve. These well-educated and cultured men and women have a lot to offer the world, and they have the ability to do a lot of good serving and leading in the military. And I feel I got a lot out of serving, personally, so I think that the benefit goes both ways.

I've also worked as an engineer in between the military and law school. I think the military is one of the very few employers that devotes itself to training people in good leadership. In most civilian occupations, leaders arise by accident. The military believes that leadership can be taught. So I think that my peers in law school would benefit enormously from having a military background. I also suspect that government officials at all levels, including members of Congress, the President, and judges and justices, would benefit from leadership training and experience.

My experience with the military was great. It's made me a better leader, and it lets me be relaxed in much of my civilian work—nothing is as stressful as some of the things I went through in the Army. The Army is also one of the most diverse institutions I've been associated with, racially and otherwise.

Most people at HLS who find out that I was in the Army are pretty positive about it. But I think there's a definite undercurrent of anti-military sentiment among some members of the student body. It's most clear with the Solomon Amendment issue/don't-ask-don't-tell [gays in the military] policy. The fliers that go up and the demonstrations that happen make it clear that they blame members of the military for the policy. It is obvious (or should be obvious) to them that your average private, sergeant, lieutenant, or colonel does not set the policy, and at most is bound to enforce it.

I think ROTC being out of favor is a holdover from Vietnam. Once open gays are allowed in the service by Congress, I don't think ROTC will be welcomed back onto campus with open arms.
Geoffrey Weien

. . . People come together through service and hard work. So many people complain about feeling isolated from their fellow humans, but don't see that sacrifice breeds connectedness. In my limited military experience, I have learned to sacrifice my own good for the good of the team, and that instills a kind of joy few of my peers have had. It doesn't matter if your face is muddy or you haven't showered in seven days—you just feel so good for being part of your unit. That is missing in America and I think it is a real tragedy.

My Ivy League peers often speak about war, peace, and peacekeeping. Many of them want to participate in the policy communities that make big decisions about those issues. But if you scratch the surface, you see that they don't know the difference between a first sergeant and a lieutenant colonel! I wonder how people can believe they should have the right to make policy choices without a working knowledge of the facts, and an understanding of the people who execute those decisions. I have explained the difference between enlisted and officer so many times at my law school—I wonder how people can make it this far and not know what an NCO is![14]

I love feeling part of the U.S. Army. Joining changed a lot of things for me, and it formed my character. I learned confidence, toughness, how to fail gracefully, how to win as a team . . . the positive experiences are priceless. I would encourage any woman who really wants to challenge herself to join.

Many of my peers in the military think or perceive that a lot of criticism and "military bashing" comes from the Ivy Leagues and the "liberal media." Actually, I would say that more big institutions (Congress, the World Bank, the Federal Reserve, etc.) need scrutiny and criticism. Distrust of power is an American virtue! I am serving to protect the Constitution, and it calls for a free press and free speech. So criticism rolls off my back, and I place it in that context. That being said, I understand that many people (military and their families,

---

14. An NCO is a noncommissioned officer—someone who came up through the enlisted ranks to a position of responsibility and leadership over other enlisted individuals. They are in many ways the heart of each service.

especially) feel hurt when they hear it. What really appalls me is the IGNORANCE in our society about the military. . . .

Active duty female Army 1st Lieutenant and former Rhodes scholar (name withheld)

THE EFFECT OF THE GAP ON THE HEALTH OF THE MILITARY

Given that military service involves a certain amount of self-sacrifice, it seems to us likely that at some point military personnel will ask: "Why should I fight and perhaps die for a bunch of rich and powerful people who never send their own sons and daughters to serve with us?" or "Why should I be in the military when everyone else thinks it is a terrible thing to do—that I'm a victim or a sucker for being here?" It is hard to fight for your country when—let's be frank—it is often not grateful. And it is hard to serve leaders whose commitment to military service ends at lip service.[15]

Those in the military who become disillusioned can solve the problem of how they feel about the wider culture by getting out en masse. That day may come. If and when it does, the left will blame Republican policy for overextending our military. And the right will

---

15. The problem has been exacerbated by the sense in the military that the fight in Iraq and elsewhere against Islamic terror, or for the attempted reshaping of the Middle East, is not shared within the country. Since 9/11 we have not had a national war effort. Our military is 0.4 percent of the population, and though it seems to be terribly understaffed, there is no serious political effort to increase the size—so that a tiny proportion of the population bears an enormous burden in this war. At the same time, the military budget is a smaller proportion of the country's gross domestic product (GDP) than it was at any time from the 1940s to the mid-'90s. We spend about 3.7 percent of our GDP on military activities today, compared to about 4.4 percent in 1993 (post–Cold War, pre–War on Terror), or to 9.2 percent, in 1962, between Korea and Vietnam. Figures from table 3.1: "Outlays by Superfunction and Function: 1940–2009," in Office of Management and Budget, *Historical Tables, Budget of the United States Government, Fiscal Year 2005* (2004) (Washington, D.C.: U.S. Government Printing Office, 2005), pp. 45–52.

blame Democrats for not supporting the war effort. Our country will be in very serious trouble whoever is to blame.

We feel that both sides of the aisle are contributing to the alienation of the military. The lack of solidarity between all classes of Americans lies at the heart of the threat of a mass departure from military service. Again this is a matter of fact and perception. We can imagine there would be a very different perception in the military about the society they are asked to sacrifice for if in most platoons there were a few men and women who came from or were headed to top colleges—and if most of our national leaders were seen welcoming home a son or daughter from duty in Afghanistan or Iraq along with other Americans.

A telling example is an experience sociologist Charles Moskos shared recently with us. In the 1990s, he spoke with a group of Army recruiters, and he asked them which they thought would aid more in their recruiting: having their budget doubled or having Chelsea Clinton enlist in the Army. Overwhelmingly, the recruiters chose the option of having a sitting president's child serve.

Kathy walked around her base neighborhood one day in the fall of 2005, talking to a number of families. She heard about a group of eleven Cobra attack helicopter pilots who had been deployed to Iraq together in 2005, all just past the midpoint of their careers in the military. Eight of them left the service after that deployment, because they frankly saw no end in sight to what the country was asking them to do—back-to-back deployments, away from families for years on end.

Their reasons for leaving were not the hard work, danger, and distance from their wives and children, but the fact that the same few military personnel were being asked to make sacrifices over and over again, while the rest of society went about their personal business, unaffected by what in any other era of our nation's history would have been a national effort. It seemed that only the military was at war, while the instructions to the rest of the country from the political leadership was to go shopping and travel so the airlines and the economy would keep on cranking.

Kathy talked to a family whose father, a supply officer, had been home just four months in the last three years because of three consecutive deployments to Iraq. It was not the tempo of operations alone that he minded; it was the sense that the country as a whole did not share the hardships. The family was unsure about whether to extend their commitment. (Yet so far, reenlistment rates have remained high.) And Kathy also met many members of the military family who had just returned home from Iraq and were asked to cut short their time with their families—sometimes after less than a few weeks at home following a seven-month deployment—and race to the gulf coast to rescue hurricane victims, patrol streets, apprehend looters, and restore order. Meanwhile for much of the rest of the country, the biggest "problem" was high gas prices or which new diet to follow.

SUSTAINING MILITARY MISSIONS

Sociologist Charles Moskos identified the problem of basic fairness (or the lack of it) as the root of whether America has the resolve to follow through with lengthy and dangerous missions. He tracked various military engagements in history and showed that "citizens accept hardship only when their elites are viewed as self-sacrificing." When elites do not serve in the military, the basic legitimacy of the mission is undermined, and the population as a whole will not continue to support it.[16]

Moskos's thesis demands the attention of senior policy makers. If it is true, our current situation puts the long-term safety of America at risk. We currently have the kind of military Moskos warns against.

---

16. Charles Moskos, "Our Will to Fight Depends on Who Is Willing to Die," *Wall Street Journal,* March 20, 2002, p. A22.

If we fail in one too many engagements, the message to America's real enemies is clear: this is a country that can't or won't follow through. Few can doubt the effect that will have on our status in the world and on the safety of our country.

The gap not only leads to a decrease in individuals being willing to serve, it may also cause an erosion of the quality of the relationship between the military and the civilians who direct it. Analyzing the TISS survey, experts Paul Gronke and Peter Feaver found that a remarkable number of respondents, both in the general public and among leadership groups, believe that if civilian leaders order the military to do something that the military opposes, then the military will seek ways to avoid doing it, at least some of the time. Almost *half* of the top professionals *without* any military experience expect, as the authors put it, "what amounts to military insubordination at least some of the time." Whether these folks realize it or not, that represents a startling amount of distrust.

The expectation of insubordination is not nearly as high among military leaders. When asked whether the military will seek to avoid following an order it opposes, two-thirds of elite military officers give the proper answer of "rarely" or "never." But nearly one-fifth of elite military officers expect the military to try to avoid orders from civilians some of the time, and that's a significant number. And a small but important 5 percent think the military will do so most or all of the time.[17]

Gronke and Feaver conclude their study noting "there is reason to worry about the differences in opinion and belief between civilian society and the military and to be vigilant about finding ways to manage it."[18] They ask whether members of the military should

---

17. Paul Gronke and Peter D. Feaver, "Uncertain Confidence: Civil and Military Attitudes about Civil-Military Relations," in Feaver and Kohn, *Soldiers and Civilians*, p. 156.
18. Ibid. p. 161.

publicly criticize a senior member of the civilian branch of government, publicly express political views just like any other citizen, and advocate military policies they believe are in the best interests of the United States, and conclude, "Elite civilian non-veterans are the most strict about restricting the military's voice in society, while elite military officers are the most strict about preserving that voice."[19]

WHO HAS THE POWER?

Our elected leaders and our cultural leaders depend on the health of the military to protect a huge array of vital interests. A military that distrusts the decision making of those civilian leaders could potentially undermine their leadership, by withholding information, tailoring actions, or otherwise acting too independently. One can hardly imagine a worse scenario in a democracy than to have an unbridgeable gap develop into an us-and-them mentality between the military and the civilian culture and leadership.

Moreover, both the military and the civilians who support it need to feel that the sacrifices asked of the military are worthwhile, or they can simply opt out. It is hard for a civilian leadership that lacks meaningful ties to the military to make the case that it has the wisdom, fairness, and commitment to make the call for those sacrifices.

---

19. Ibid., p. 159.

7. Why Do We Even Need the Military?

★★★★★★★★★★★★★★★★★★★★

The right thing is to honor our oaths. The right thing to do is to make the part of the conflict we touch as good as we can. To bring good to an evil situation; to cradle and feed the orphans; to destroy those who are given to evil; to tend the wounds of an enemy soldier; to smile at a group of scared civilians.

—Major John J. Thomas USAF

For the foreseeable future America is going to be the great world power. And this reality affects all Americans, no matter what our politics or economic status. It affects the economics of our daily life, and the risks we face. As we write, all Americans are considered targets by a group of Islamic extremists holding views fatally antithetical to ours. And there is no reason to believe the situation will remain static. Between writing these lines and the time it takes to publish them, the country could be facing heretofore unimagined new challenges. Our nation is vulnerable, powerful, and obligated.

The person who volunteers for military service today is volunteering, among other things, to maintain the fighting capability of the United States military, carrying the torch so that it may stay lit five, ten, twenty, or a hundred years from now. This tradition is jeopardized by the idea that all need not share the burdens of those who wear a uniform or that policy disagreements are an excuse to opt out.

Frank

While John was at war, I went up to Harlem one day to listen to the old guys play jazz. I was looking for Seleno Clarke. Seleno, a big man with a friendly, fleshy, craggy face, is one of the "old jazz guys" I met at Smoke, the jazz club a few blocks from my apartment.

Seleno and I had been sitting at the bar of Anna's Restaurant eating bean soup and drinking wine when he told me that he hosts a jam session every Sunday at the American Legion post in Harlem. He said that the Legion is always "filled with vets and jazz but no egos; I don't allow that; everybody gets a turn when we jam. It's where it's happening, man, not the Blue Note but the Legion post, that's right."

Seleno wrote the address on a napkin: 132nd Street between Seventh and Eighth. He did this after I told him my son was a Marine in combat overseas. A few days later Seleno gave me a CD to send John. He signed it, and under his signature wrote: "To John Schaeffer, USMC. Thanks, brother."

I went to hear the jazz John loves in the company of his fellow veterans. It was a way to hear great music, the very heart of the best art my country has created, and to feel close to my son while he was far away in Afghanistan trying to kill or catch the people who had been part of a plot to murder thousands of New Yorkers not far from where I was sitting.

Standing room only, about eighty people packed into a space the size of an average living room; some eating off heaped paper plates full of fried codfish, chicken, and meat loaf, everyone else clutching a drink. The crowd was jammed around five or so small tables under a low ceiling. Seleno was playing his beloved Hammond B-3 organ and launching into his signature tune, "Harlem Groove," feet flying on the pedals, pounding out the chest-compressing base notes, while his big hands caressed the tune. I signed in, glancing at the wall-to-wall handsome black women, most middle-aged, some older, a few younger, a few wearing 1930s- and 1940s-style fur coats and fancy hats, in a lovely tribute to the "Jazz Age." There were several nerdy white kids in sweats who had brought their instruments to jam and lots of old black guys wearing American Legion, World War II, Korean War, and Vietnam War vet baseball caps.

After the set, Seleno walked my way hugging and greeting everyone he passed. Then it was my turn. Seleno folded me in his arms. He turned to a sax player who looked as if he was about ninety.

"His son is a Marine and is over there!" Seleno shouted through the din.

One of the grizzled black guys in a Legion baseball cap stepped over and asked if I was okay. Seleno introduced the man as the commander of the post and told him about John. Then the Legion post president took the mike off the stand.

"Hush, I said HUSH!" he said in a raspy voice.

Almost everyone got quiet.

"We have a brother with us here tonight whose son is over there fighting for you and me. His son is a Marine. For God and country, brother, for God and country! Bless you!"

"Semper Fi!" someone shouted.

Several regal women in long fur coats surged toward me. Old men shook my hand. The white kids looked everywhere but at me.

They had come here for jazz. What on earth was *this* all about? Then the president of the post stepped up to the mike again.

"Thank your son, brother. God bless him and God bless America."

Seleno kicked into "Misty," and a couple of the old black guys bought me a drink.

I lost myself in the music while thinking about the fact that this American Legion post was filled with men who served back in the days of a segregated military, when black men had to struggle for the right to serve with honor, when white DIs called them "ink spots" and insulted them or worse, when they had to struggle to be allowed the "privilege" of combat duty. I thought about the indignities so many black Americans put up with so I can be free. And I thought about the fact that America is a great nation that does not accept the status quo, but struggles to become better, fairer. And sometimes things do change for the better. My son was in a military where he was a brother to these veterans, their son and grandson now as much as he was my flesh and blood. I thought about one of the Marines my son admired most, his African American senior drill instructor, an "awesome Marine," as John always said.

The next time I was up at the Legion post in Harlem, I made it a point to get there early and go around and shake a lot of hands, and say thank you to a lot of "strangers" for their service. The African Americans who served in the not-so-distant past provide the ultimate example of putting the good of our country ahead of self. For if ever any Americans had the right to turn their backs on their country, it was the greatest generation of African Americans. Instead, they served willingly, even when our country betrayed that service thorough segregation and racism. And their vote of confidence in our country, during World War I, World War II, and beyond is one reason my son came home alive from two back-to-back combat tours.

As I said, John's senior drill instructor, Staff Sergeant George Henderson, is black (something I remarked on after I met him, and John, a color-blind Marine, had not mentioned), and the discipline, self-confidence, and knowledge he instilled in John brought John through combat. John's drill instructors were part of a tradition of service that taught my son to look out for others ahead of self, to, if need be, lay down his life for the Marine or soldier standing next to him. In our book *Keeping Faith,* John wrote:

> Only at the end of training did we realize how many hours and days our DIs had put into us without eating or sleeping, so that we could become what we wanted to be. One DI had worked one hundred and sixty hours our first week on the Island. (There are only one hundred and sixty-eight hours in a week!) He had had so little time to eat that he had lost forty pounds in our first month of training. (He was not fat to begin with.) It was this way with all of our DIs. They broke themselves for us. They could have earned more flipping burgers. I felt grateful to them. They had led from the front, going step for step with us and for us.
>
> Only at the end did we truly appreciate how much our DIs had given us. They regarded our transformation into Marines as a life mission worthy of many sacrifices and pains that we could hardly understand and were just beginning to appreciate. They had demanded a great deal of us and twice as much of themselves.

The role of the military is not only to fight today's wars but also to pass on a tradition of excellence and discipline while preparing for what may come. John's senior drill instructor and other DIs had not known what war they were preparing my son for. All they knew in the summer of 1999 was that they would do their best to produce the best Marines they could. And the other volunteers in John's platoon had not signed up to fight in any particular war. They joined to become Marines because their country had asked them to, whatever their individual and personal reasons at the time.

In the summer of 2004, five years after John went through boot camp, I sought out Staff Sergeant Henderson (just retired) and interviewed him for several hours one morning, sitting in the library at Camp Lejeune. I was trying to figure out what made exemplary Marines tick. I asked Henderson why he joined: "I was sixteen when I went down to the recruiters' office. It was heaven to me. They treated me differently—they were professionals. It was something to find professional men. I had never seen this. I never saw that in my father or my uncles. I'd never seen a man who was professional about what he did and treated other people with that kind of respect."

I asked Henderson about how he dealt with such a diverse population of recruits during the time he was a DI.

> They might start out in racial cliques, with the black kids hanging together and the white kids hanging together, but at boot camp you figure how to level it all out. What you do is you have to destroy all those differences. You have to show them there is a better way and it's to be a team. That's the point. "This is my family" is how you want them to think. And they do. When you put on a campaign cover [the "Smokey Bear" hat worn by drill instructors], you are either a green belt or a black belt or "Nick the new hat." Those are the only "races" here.[1]
>
> If you're not a mentor, what are you doing? Out of everything I've ever done, the most meaningful thing in my life was being a senior drill instructor. I had an opportunity to

---

1. Junior DIs wear a green belt; the senior DIs a black belt. "Nick, the new hat" is slang for a first-time DI."

do something greater than a college professor ever does, even greater than some recruits' parents can do. I had an impact on the lives of my Marines out of all proportion to their time spent in boot camp. I could see the change.

George Henderson had made Marines. Whether or not he ever fought in a war, he fulfilled one of the central missions of his service—to provide continuity.

Kathy

Not everyone believes we need a military. Some people are quite sure we do not. My oldest friend, Sam, for instance, is a pacifist and an anarchist. We've been friends since I moved in across the street from his house in second grade. We were friends through high school, where he sported a "Question Authority" button and where we would debate issues like the nature of consciousness at our cafeteria lunch table. In college, Sam started wearing his hair longer than mine; in his senior year he spent one hundred days in jail for trespassing on the grounds of General Dynamics.

Sam's got a point of view. He explained to me once that two people walking down the street from opposite directions would walk around each other—they do not need the state to tell them not to bump heads. He lives his point of view, working for the pacifist American Friends Service Committee, serving as a board member of the venerable, pre–World War II secular-pacifist War Resisters League, and counseling soldiers on how to get out of their military commitments for reasons of conscience. He's been with Valerie, his partner, almost twenty years now, and they have a son together, but they haven't married because Sam sees coercion in the state's involvement in a relationship. I thought when I married Greg that it might end my friendship with Sam but it didn't. Sam is antiwar and anti-military. But he's not anti-anybody.

Sam wrote me one of the more touching e-mails I received during Greg's first deployment to Iraq. He wrote:

> I know that you, and perhaps Greg, might disagree with me about some policy issues related to this war. Overall, I'm saddened that the world was not able to muster enough support for nonviolent efforts to overthrow Saddam Hussein. I'm upset that those of us in the peace movement in the U.S. were not able to convince enough people in the U.S. to stop the U.S. government from ordering Greg to participate in, witness, and endure the tragedies of war. I'd like to apologize to him for not being able to successfully prevent the government from ordering him into battle.
> Peace,
> Sam

Sam believes that we ought never resort to war for any reason, that reaching out with compassion and conscience will always be better than force. We disagree. But I respect his perspective, and think it has something to offer—and I want a world without war too.

I respect Sam, because, after all, he could be right and I could be wrong. I appreciate that he was willing to argue for his case and take responsibility for not convincing others—a responsibility I wish more partisans would take. In my mind, Sam is excused from advocating what Frank and I advocate here, equal class representation in the military, because he wants no one to serve. He is willing to live with any repercussion that comes from disbanding our military. Short of having a perspective like Sam's, though, there is little moral ground for abstaining from this discussion.

I've seen some of the places in the world with weak government, and without security. In my mid-twenties I went as a traveler and a nominal freelance journalist to Colombia. I rode on the tops of ancient buses through Andean villages where the government did not reach and drug traffickers and paramilitary groups battled for control. I shared a little pensione with some middle-class grave robbers, who dug up burial sites and peddled what they found. I went to a soccer game with a young drug-traffic investigator I interviewed, and watched him chase down and beat up a purse snatcher, only to let him go, because it would be too much of a bother to take him into custody. I interviewed many brave Colombians who were trying to wrest control of their country back from lawless elements, and I've noted with sadness over the years as most of them have been assassinated. I did have a sense, in my travels, that I was protected because I was American. I felt lucky to return home.

I have seen a lot of evidence that the world has many strangers in it who would not politely "walk around each other" if they were to meet on a deserted sidewalk, with no outside order to constrain them. In many places in the world, murder, rape, or robbery would be the result of such an encounter. I'm with Joseph Conrad: I believe the veneer of civilization is very thin; we need to do all we can to keep it intact.

Frank and Kathy

You don't have to share our point of view to buy into the argument we are making: we need a strong military and it is the duty of all classes to be involved in making it so. In fact, we don't necessarily agree on how the country should use the military, or what the threats and opportunities are in the world. One could believe that the American government is in the pocket of wealthy corporations, and our argument should still resonate. In that scenario, the children of the privileged would be a damper on reckless action. One could believe that America is a "city set on a hill" and that we need to use force to spread democracy. In that scenario, the children of privilege should do their part. In fact, the only worldview exempt from our logic is that of Kathy's friend Sam. And there aren't many authentic Sams.

Without America's military presence not only Americans would feel the loss, but fewer Frenchmen would be exporting wine, fewer Koreans would be exporting cars, and it would be rare for a tourist to visit New York from India (and vice versa). We take a certain level of U.S.-imposed stability for granted, even our enemies and loudest international critics do.

Any student of history knows that there has always been a great power or a combination of powers regionally or globally. The British, the Spanish, the Chinese, and many others have had their day and may again someday emerge as the guarantors of stability. For the past sixty-odd years, America has been a great power.

Since the end of the Cold War, while America has continued to patrol the world, the number of armed conflicts globally and the number of people worldwide dying because of war are the lowest they have ever been in history.[2] This may be coincidence—it may not be.

In the stunning movie *Hotel Rwanda* there is a poignant scene. A corrupt Rwandan general who is doing nothing to save a group of Tutsi refugees about to be slaughtered by the Hutu forces has a change of heart and provides some desperately needed, albeit temporary protection to the persecuted minority. His change of heart comes about because he is told that "the Americans" are watching the slaughter with spy satellites. He is told: "The Americans know everything; they will be coming."

The general does not know if the threat is true—tragically it wasn't. But he does know that "the Americans" do tend to show up

2. *Human Security Report 2005,* available online at http://www.humansecurityreport. info.

around the globe and make people like Hitler, Milosevic, Gadhafi, and Saddam Hussein accountable. It is a powerful moment at the heart of a wrenching film. And it makes a subtle point that has nothing to do with the story: the very existence of the powerful U.S. military has often been a stabilizing force in the world, its misuses and mistakes notwithstanding.

American military power gives weight to the words of American presidents, as a stick but as a carrot too. For instance, President Kennedy was able to persuade the Saudi royal family to abolish slavery and free tens of thousands of their slaves in 1963. How? It was not just his compelling moral argument; it was because he was the commander in chief of the military that was guaranteeing open sea-lanes and the Saudi ability to export oil.

GUNS AND BUTTER

So what is the nature of the jobs for which the nation's military prepares? Broadly understood, the military's purpose can be seen in terms of muscle, goods, order, and good. Some missions will bring two or more of these aspects into play.

Muscle. The Department of Defense asserts that the purpose of the military is to fight and win the nation's wars. The term that they give to soldiers, sailors, airmen, Coast Guardsmen, and Marines is "warfighters," to make that clear. Yet, an underlying theory here is that credible preparation prevents war. A soldier's purpose is no more to "make" war than the job of a crime fighter is to make crime. We won the Cold War because of the bankruptcy of the communist system compared to ours, and without another great European war, which almost certainly would have happened without the power of our military and its alliances. We know from Soviet archives that they understood we had been willing to turn the Cold War hot in Korea, Vietnam, and the Cuban Missile Crisis, and that affected their actions. Perhaps we won the peace because freedom works better than tyranny and corresponds more closely to human nature and aspirations. But we prevented a war because each generation of our military passed down a tradition of service and we had lethal power our enemies knew we could and would use.

Defense is fundamental to the purpose of government. Whoever the president and whatever platform he is elected on, once he takes office he is likely to find, as Alexander Hamilton said, that safety from external danger is "the most powerful director of national conduct."[3]

Goods. The military protects our economic well-being as well. The protection of maritime commerce remains vital today, when so much of our economic life is truly global in scope. We still rely on the Navy and other members of the military to ensure that goods that cross the seas to foreign ports do so unmolested (whether we are as aware of it as Americans were one hundred years ago or not). Key routes, in places such as the Strait of Malacca in Indonesia, are still infested with pirates who will seize ships and cargo, absent a protective presence. And in the age of Islamic terror that spans the world from Morocco to Indonesia this job is more complex and difficult than ever. The very fact of the existence of American naval power keeps many countries from even contemplating the use of their regional power to place a choke hold on world commerce. Most Americans take for granted the fact that goods and services can flow around the world unmolested. This is a tremendous tribute to the effectiveness of American naval power.

Order. The military has been called on to help bring order to other countries. When the military conducts "security and stabilization" missions in Africa, for instance, it is hoping to quell the

---

3. Alexander Hamilton, James Madison, and John Jay, *The Federalist Papers* (New York: Signet Classic, 2003) p. 61.

anarchy that precludes economic development. When the government sends the military on humanitarian missions or to train foreign militaries, it may be seeking to build diplomatic relations with these countries, to lessen the likelihood of instability or friction in the future.

The military enforces agreements as well. As any lawmaker (or parent) knows, without an enforcement mechanism, no rule or agreement is likely to survive. In the anarchy of states' relations with one another, the military is a key mechanism for enforcement of our treaties or U.N. rulings.

Good. The U.S. military has become the humanitarian response of choice for the world's worst disasters, from the tsunami in East Asia to the earthquake in Pakistan to Hurricane Katrina here at home, three huge efforts in 2005 alone. The U.S. military has been in every region of the globe on humanitarian missions that range from building roads and schools to ending mass starvation. The military is *the* organization with the discipline, skill, and resources to bring order to chaos, hope to desperate situations. In this role, the U.S. military has literally saved hundreds of thousands of lives that were at imminent risk.

Although the military must follow its civilian leaders, whose inconsistency can frequently make it difficult for the soldier to construct a coherent narrative from their actions, the military institution and its members continue to struggle to place their own actions in an ethical context.[4] Military purpose and conduct are rooted in a moral conception, which derives from the founding documents of our country. Commanders' courses at U.S. military war colleges all include seminal texts on ethics, just-war theory, constitutional action, and philosophy.

---

4. For more on this topic, see Anthony Hartle, *Moral Issues in Military Decision-Making* (Kansas: University Press of Kansas, 1990).

THE RELATIONSHIP BETWEEN THE MILITARY AND THE STATE

Regardless of its missions or purpose, the military does not act in its own name, but in the name of America. One of the great struggles of ideas in America today is the question of what constitutes American national security: How should we use our military and other instruments of international affairs? How can we best be safe, promote our interests and the interests of the world? Out of the many schools of thought, we can perhaps distill four main foreign-policy perspectives that compete for primacy today. They are neo-isolationism, realism, neoconservatism, and global integrationism. Individual Americans may not necessarily know the names of the different schools of thought, but they tend to subscribe, more or less, to one school or another.

Realism was the dominant theory behind the Cold War and, according to some researchers of military affairs, tends to be the philosophy most hewed to by senior military officials. Realism is described by an observation often ascribed to Benjamin Disraeli, the great nineteenth-century British prime minister: a country has no permanent friends or permanent enemies, only permanent interests. Realism sees the international scene primarily as relations between nations, who act in their national self-interest, going to war only when vital national interests are at stake. Proponents of this view would be less likely to support operations other than war.

Neoconservatism has been the reigning philosophy of the United States during most of the George W. Bush presidency. Neoconservatism holds that America is a force for good in the world based on our core American principles of freedom, free enterprise, equality, and democracy. As such, America should encourage the spread of our system and values for the good of the world and our nation, and must confront the foreign evil in the world, because it will eventually threaten us directly if we do not. It believes that armed coercion is the most effective tool against that evil.

Isolationism, or perhaps neo-isolationism, is the proposition that America should concern itself with immediate issues of homeland security and scale back our international involvements to avoid imperial overstretch. It argues that we should make common defense the center of our military policy and use force as a last resort requiring congressional approval before any international interaction as a dampening force, enhance U.S. strategic self-sufficiency, limit U.S. defense spending, we should enhance alternative instruments of statecraft, revive the concept of citizen soldier, and eliminate the military academies.[5]

Finally, the school of *global integrationism,* or integrated power, sees the goal of national security as being to protect the American people, prevent conflict through engagement, and lead modernized international institutions. Integrationists seek to combine the hard and soft power of the Department of Homeland Security, the State Department, the Commerce Department, the CIA, the Pentagon, the FBI, the Treasury, and the U.S. Trade Representative's Office as parts of a single whole.

Whatever disagreements proponents of these schools of thought have with one another, they all provide support for broad citizen participation in our military. Realism would support broad participation of the leadership's children in the military, since their presence would likely cause the national leaders to focus clearly on whether a given engagement involves the country's vital interests. Neoconservatism would promote the idea of the country's leadership classes serving, because that service would reinforce the message of some of the

---

5. Bacevich, *New American Militarism,* pp. 205–226.

strengths of America—its equality and that its espoused principles represent the views of all classes of society. Isolationism explicitly supports the involvement of privileged children in the military, which it sees as a damper on adventurism. And integrated-power proponents want an educated military capable of complex tasks, one that presumably would benefit from the service of the children of the most educated classes.

Most Americans view our national interests abroad in terms of a combination of these schools. Again, other than the alternative of principled and consistent pacifism, there is no mainstream political philosophy of the exercise of American power and our nation's defenses that does not depend on a viable and cohesive military. That means, in our view, that almost every American has a practical but also a moral stake in our military, whatever disagreements they might have with a given policy or politician.

THE SOLDIER AND THE STATE

Frank received a copy of this letter from an Air Force officer, describing his job as he sees it. We feel his letter exactly lays out what we are trying to say about the fact that no matter what school of thought we Americans subscribe to, the role of the military is not only vital but, seen from the point of view of the individual soldier, one that depends on trust in our democracy. The officer wrote this letter from Iraq to his family.

> ... None of us can be sure if we understand, on the grand scale, what actions are right—like our country going to war. We can trust and pray that our leaders are acting ethically. But even they have to make decisions without omniscience, with their human intellect. ...
>
> So we are left, all of us, not just those in the military, to

act as best we can to do good given the circumstances we are put in. Just like anything else, in the military it is more a series of decisions. You find yourself in a situation and are faced with acting within the situation. You wake up each day and do your job.

It goes something like this, we think: Is it right to defend freedom? Then we raise our hands and swear to do so by joining the military. And at that point we also pledge to follow "the president of the United States and those appointed above us." Is it right to go to war? No one is asking us. We follow the decisions of the elected officials who represent the will and wisdom of the American people. What they ask us to do is fight that war—morally, without malice, without giving in to evil. We are asked to follow the "law of armed conflict" by not shooting at medical operations and by not targeting civilians, and such. We conduct the war and try to spare lives by ending it quickly.

So we get orders to go to Iraq, and we go. The right thing is to honor our oaths. The right thing to do is to make the part of the conflict we touch as good as we can. To, with prayer, bring good to an evil situation; to cradle and feed the orphans; to destroy those who are given to evil; to tend the wounds of an enemy soldier; to smile at a group of scared civilians; to be a Good Samaritan. What we do even unto the "least of these . . ."

When you're someplace across the world, you don't feel you're a world away. It becomes your daily life, and you act just as you might if you were back home and saw someone with a flat tire and stopped to help, or if someone were trying to kill your neighbor and you had the means to stop them. You don't think every minute about the grand scale of things. You do what you can to be good where you are.

That's not so much courage, that's focusing on doing what

you are there to do. You've given your oath. If you weren't doing it, someone else would be, and you'd rather be there trying to do good than have someone else there who might not. The courage comes when having to leave your family at the airport. The rest is just trying your best to get through the days until you are with them again.

Major John J. Thomas USAF

8. What If We Don't Fix the Problem?

★★★★★★★★★★★★★★★★★★★★

*Do we need more people from the upper classes of society
in the military? Even if there is a benefit to maintaining
a representative military, I'm not sure it would be worth
the cost.*

—Lieutenant Colonel Michael Strobl, USMC

We have argued that, ultimately, the U.S. military acts as the expression of the American people. It is an exemplar of who we are in the world, whether we wish it to be or not. And yet—when it comes to military service there is a mutually reinforcing relationship between the "leave-it-to-us-professionals" attitude of some of our military leaders and the "leave-me-alone" or "not-with-my-child" attitude of many in the upper classes.

With the Vietnam experience still resonating in the military, there are some people who seem to prefer being part of a "profession of arms"—set apart from the distractions of civilian life and perhaps the political repercussions that would go with a more truly representative force. "Just let us do our job" seems to sum up the attitude. If we need more recruits, let's not recast the debate, let's just do more of the same—find 'em where we already find 'em, keep 'em as long as we can.

After all, the news for recruiters is not that bad.[1] Why panic? Why panic, indeed, echoes the privileged parent. We can solve the small problem of recruiting without involving my child, surely?

Our national leadership seems likewise unperturbed. Within Washington's marble halls, there seems to be little sense that we need to change. The upper classes, the government, and many in the military seem satisfied.

Kathy

Privileged culture involves lots of things that are appealing. Stone Barns, for example, is an idyllic, grassy showplace for organic food and sustainable farming built on the Rockefeller estate in Westchester County, New York, the sort of beautifully reimagined vision of a farm that could be created only by people with money and taste and high ideals. Julie, an old school friend, and I were strolling the grounds there with our children one day, on a bit of a retreat from day-to-day deployment life.

We bumped into a good friend of hers, a former art magazine editor. Julie explained that my husband was in Iraq. Julie's friend gave me her full attention, answering her own question by nodding while saying, "He's a journalist?"

"No," I said. "He's a Marine."

You could almost see the wheels turn as she sought to reorient herself. Her eyes stayed on mine, but her expression flattened out from engaged to uneasy. She seemed to be searching for the right thing to say. It reminded me of what I'd read in a book called *The Etiquette of*

---

1. *New York Times,* July 13, 2005, (AP) "Initiative Opposes Military Recruiting on Campus."

Illness on how ill people often need to help their well acquaintances to deal with the fact of illness.[2] Finally, in a low voice with a bit of a tragic edge, she said slowly, "That must be very hard." And the conversation continued a bit, her feeling her way on the narrow rocky edge of the subject, and me trying to convey that it really was okay.

My purpose is not to criticize this very nice woman. She was trying to be sympathetic. But it was clearly a collision of expectations and cultures—in this place, among the high, rustic stone arches and fat hens, she did not expect to confront the issue of someone fighting a war. And so it is, too, with most of the people who visit lovely Stone Barns, I imagine. Their lives do not touch those of people who serve in the military, and they certainly never consider the actual experience of serving.

My friend Julie is not uncomfortable with Greg's serving, nor are so many of my friends and family members who have been wonderfully supportive when Greg was deployed. Some called out of the blue to see how I was; a good number are like Julie, who is sympathetic and grateful for what Greg does even though it falls well outside of her life experience as a psychologist, mother, and wife of a Wall Street banker. Friends often tell me they have a different perspective now, a different sensibility about the war and the idea of military service from the one they had before they knew Greg. Not necessarily better or worse, but different.

It strikes me that wittingly or not, members of the military family are emissaries from the front line of government policy to the people safely ensconced within America's borders. Military families can create a feedback loop that can reinforce support or quicken the rejection of a government policy. We military families with nonmilitary ties humanize those troops for many Americans and, in the process, perhaps both make it matter more how those

---

2. Susan P. Halpern, *The Etiquette of Illness* (New York: Bloomsbury, 2004).

troops are used and give people more faith in who those troops actually are.

If those on the military front lines report to their circles that things are going well, that they see more good than bad, morale is high, they, the soldiers, have faith in our ability to do our mission—then they convey something important. If they say something less positive, that is important information too. Without that feedback loop, it seems to me, the legitimacy of the government's actions suffer.

Frank

I have several old nonmilitary friends who do get it. One such person is Frank Gruber, who, as John was heading out to the Middle East on his first combat deployment, e-mailed me the following message, one of the most sensible, practical, and compassionate notes of encouragement I got from anyone:

> . . . I know I don't understand what you're going through with him over there—I know it's not the same thing as sending Henry [Frank G's then-thirteen-year-old son] off to beach camp. You just have to look at it statistically. If he'd never joined the Marines, he'd be in some danger if he was [just] hanging out . . . or at some college somewhere. He's living his life.

Frank is proof to me that you can disagree with policy—Frank is a smart, lefty Democrat and deeply involved in Santa Monica local politics—and yet not be anti-military. Frank vehemently opposed the Iraq war from the start. And yet he speaks of our military with the greatest respect. But Frank has also told me that knowing my family and knowing John in particular has somewhat changed the way he looks at our military.

Frank Gruber's responses and his relationship to our military, as seen through the lens of my experience, prove three things to me. First: even someone as intelligent and naturally kind as Frank will not have real empathy with our men and women without some personal contact, or what Kathy calls the "feedback loop." Second: my friendship with Frank makes me think that some military people are perhaps too quick to write off "all those left-wing Democrats" when it comes to support for our military. Third: the feedback loop works both ways. I am totally invested in my children. Their friends are my friends. Frank admires my son's military service so I'm ready to forgive just about any policy disagreements Frank and I might have. So, having at least one Frank Gruber in the life of a member of the military family is just as important as the nonmilitary person's having a real connection with those who serve. As a military parent, I can't be alienated by the bogeyman of the "Hollywood liberal" as described by right-wing radio talk show hosts, because I know and love one, actually a lot more than one, but knowing just Frank would do.

Kathy and Frank

Despite the occasional troop shortage—tied to the "popularity" of any one engagement—many military people still maintain that we shouldn't mix military personnel and larger issues of society. We asked Lieutenant Colonel Michael Strobl, who runs one of the offices that oversee personnel for the Marine Corps, to offer us the crux of the argument against broadening the spectrum of those who serve. He very kindly took the time needed to help us out. We have excerpted his summary here.

Do we need more people from the upper classes of society in the military? Even if there is a benefit to maintaining a representative military, I'm not sure it would be worth the cost.

The armed forces do not reflect the general population in many ways. For instance, males, conservatives, the able-bodied, and the young are disproportionate in the military compared with the general population. We tolerate those differences, why not class? After all, we don't think the demographic makeup of the Congress, the police department, or the department of history at Harvard University reflects the general society. Why should the military?

No one was forced to join our All-Volunteer Force. Service members are compensated for their service, and since we are an All-Volunteer Force, we can safely assume that all service members are being paid at a level above their reservation wage.[3] Perhaps the lack of socioeconomic diversity actually *enhances* readiness. It's possible that the middle class make better soldiers.

Even if society does gain by an increased cross-class shared experience as well as by having more militarily experienced policy makers, reporters, teachers, voters, are we willing to maintain a military primarily to address such social issues? Warfighting capabilities have to be the primary focus of our military. Its mission is too important for us to believe otherwise.

In fact, society may suffer a net loss of efficiency or utility if the upper classes were more represented in the military. Frequently, those who make up the upper classes of our society do so because they are simply incredibly talented. This is especially true in our American society notable for its class mobility. Would society currently be better or worse off if, say, Bill Gates had served four years as an infantryman or John Grisham three years as a helicopter mechanic before pursuing their incredibly productive and societal-enriching civilian careers?

And society would lose an important avenue of mobility

---

3. *Reservation wage:* the minimum wage required to induce an individual to work for a particular employer. For a given job, the reservation wage will be a different amount for each individual.

for the lower classes. Any effort to increase representation of one class requires a reduction in representation of another class. In other words you will end up refusing to allow certain people to join the service even though they are willing *and* perceive military service to be their *best employment option.* Is this unintended consequence a positive outcome?

Finally, any effort to change the socioeconomic makeup of the service would have costs. How would you do it? Increasing military pay would raise taxes or raise government debt burden or force reductions in other government services, or some combination of the three. Is this a positive outcome?

Conscription infringes on individual liberty and creates a military of reluctant soldiers. It is generally inefficient for society to force otherwise (nonmilitarily) talented people into the service. Society loses out on whatever else they could've been producing.

In our view, people who hold the status quo perspective just summarized seem to regard the military as just another specialized institution, comparable to other specialized civilian institutions. This "corporate" view of the military was expressed by a military spokesperson in the context of the extraordinary measures the Army was considering to meet recruiting targets in 2005–06. According to Lieutenant Colonel Bryan Hilferty, an Army personnel spokesman at the Pentagon, "A good economy and low unemployment makes it more difficult for every organization to recruit, and we are competing with all these other organizations for the best and the brightest."

Our argument is that the United States military is *not,* and should not ever be, like other large major corporations. Its success is measured not by stock trading values but by the health and continued existence of our country. And it represents all of us, to our credit or our shame, depending on how the military does its job. To own that credit, or repair the shame, it is incumbent on us to be in some way actively vested. The stance of the Army, as expressed in that quote, sells the military short by reducing what service offers to nothing more than a job or educational opportunity. It is also nonsense in light of the very real sacrifices people in the military are asked to make. One does not ask people to risk their lives, for instance, just to open another business franchise.

CLASS INTEGRATION SUPPORTS THE MISSION

The military has a tough mission. We understand the argument Lieutenant Colonel Strobl summarized for us. But military missions are both short-term—today's mission—and long-term—tomorrow's mission. Our troops provide feedback to society, and vice versa. When that feedback does not flow to those in leadership positions in a personal way, then the country stands to lose—in proper support to the troops, in weighing the stakes of suggested military actions, and in getting information from on the ground rather than from the media only. This two-way feedback is often subtle, but it is real. Multiplied across society, it can make an enormous impact. It is to the military's advantage to have as many broad and varied personal contacts with the civilian population as possible. This is what gives the military a human face to the nonmilitary population. This is what protects the military from being overused or misused by political leaders. This is what the future success of long-term military commitments will depend on.

The framers of our Constitution had good reasons for believing that an integrated military was necessary for democratic life. We no more want a military of distinct "professionals" disconnected from our larger culture than we want one successful class of Americans exempted from paying any taxes. Moreover, from the point of view of those who serve, we submit, being out of sight and therefore out of mind when it comes to our elites is not in their best interest. Perhaps being an invisible force makes war both too easy and too hard. "Get the military to solve it" is a mantra that is spoken too easily by people who don't have any personal connection to the men and women who will be called upon. And absent the widespread support that comes only from a sense of fair-shared sacrifice, costly, yet necessary long-term engagements might become politically impossible. That can lead to hasty bad planning, doing war "on the cheap." It is the military man or woman who pays the highest price for this.

We pride ourselves on being a fair country. And when something smacks of basic unfairness or, worse, when unfairness is tacitly institutionalized, it seems downright un-American and therefore suspect. People may not think this out, but their gut reaction is right. And as our leaders lose credibility in times of unpopular wars, they may earn their troubles if they have no personal connection to wars they are sending other people to fight in.

The grunt on the ground is best equipped, best trained, and best served when the opinion makers have a personal stake in his or her well-being. We submit that the best planning for warfighting is not done by political leaders who are in a hurry to "get it over" before the political winds shift, because support for a war is not deep and shared by all. It is time for a midcourse correction in the policy of the all-volunteer military and how it recruits.

We offer the following as an example how a member of the opinion-making class is affected, and hence how this discourse is affected, when a person has that personal connection. Eliot Cohen is among the most prominent and widely quoted experts in international affairs; he is a professor at the Nitze School of Advanced International Studies at Johns Hopkins (SAIS), and although he considers himself an Independent, he is often associated with neoconservatives or conservatives. He wrote a *Washington Post* op-ed as his son was preparing to ship off to Iraq in July of 2005, acknowledging a new perspective born of having a son in the service. We believe this is an important American document.

War forces us, or should force us, to ask hard questions of ourselves. As a military historian, a commentator on current events and the father of a young Army officer, these are mine.

You supported the Iraq war when it was launched in 2003. If you had known then what you know now, would you still have been in favor of it?

As I watched President Bush give his speech at Fort Bragg to rally support for the war the other week, I contemplated this question from a different vantage than my usual professorial perch. Our oldest son now dresses like the impassive soldiers who served as stage props for that event; he too wears crossed rifles, jump wings and a Ranger tab. Before long he will fight in the war that I advocated, and that the president was defending. . . .

But a pundit should not recommend a policy without adequate regard for the ability of those in charge to execute it, and here I stumbled. I could not imagine, for example, that the civilian and military high command would treat "Phase IV"—the post-combat period that has killed far more Americans than the "real" war—as of secondary importance to the planning of Gen. Tommy Franks's blitzkrieg. I never dreamed that Ambassador Paul Bremer and Gen. Ricardo Sanchez, the two top civilian and military leaders early in the occupation of Iraq—brave, honorable and committed though they were—would be so unsuited for their tasks, and that they would serve their full length of duty nonetheless.

Your son is an infantry officer, shipping out soon for Iraq. How do you feel about that?

Pride, of course—great pride. And fear. And an occasional

burning in the gut, a flare of anger at empty pieties and lame excuses, at flip answers and a lack of urgency, at a failure to hold those at the top to the standards of accountability that the military system rightly imposes on subalterns.

It is a flicker of rage that two years into an insurgency, we still expose our troops in Humvees to the blasts of road-side bombs—knowing that even the armored version of that humble successor to the Jeep is simply not designed for warfare along guerrilla-infested highways, while, at the same time, knowing that plenty of countries manufacture armored cars that are. It is disbelief at a manpower system that, following its prewar routines, ships soldiers off to war for a year or 15 months, giving them two weeks of leave at the end, when our British comrades, more experienced in these matters and wiser in pacing themselves, ship troops out for half that time, and give them an extra month on top of their regular leave after an operational deployment.

It is the sick feeling that churned inside me at least 18 months ago, when a glib and upbeat Pentagon bureaucrat assured me that the opposition in Iraq consisted of "5,000 bitter enders and criminals," even after we had killed at least that many. It flames up when hearing about the veteran who in theory has a year between Iraq rotations, but in fact, because he transferred between units after returning from one tour, will go back to Iraq half a year later, and who, because of "stop-loss orders" involuntarily extending active duty tours, will find himself in combat nine months after his enlistment runs out. And all this because after 9/11, when so many Americans asked for nothing but an opportunity to serve, we did not expand our Army and Marine Corps when we could, even though we knew we would need more troops.

A variety of emotions wash over me as I reflect on our Iraq

war: Disbelief at the length of time it took to call an insurgency by its name. Alarm at our continuing failure to promote at wartime speed the colonels and generals who have a talent for fighting it, while also failing to sweep aside those who do not. Incredulity at seeing decorations pinned on the chests and promotions on the shoulders of senior leaders—both civilians and military—who had the helm when things went badly wrong. Disdain for the general who thinks Job One is simply whacking the bad guys and who, ever conscious of public relations, cannot admit that American soldiers have tortured prisoners or, in panic, killed innocent civilians. Contempt for the ghoulish glee of some who think they were right in opposing the war, and for the blithe disregard of the bungles by some who think they were right in favoring it. A desire—barely controlled—to slap the highly educated fool who, having no soldier friends or family, once explained to me that mistakes happen in all wars, and that the casualties are not really all that high and that I really shouldn't get exercised about them.

There is a lot of talk these days about shaky public support for the war. That is not really the issue. Nor should cheerleading, as opposed to truth-telling, be our leaders' chief concern. If we fail in Iraq—and I don't think we will—it won't be because the American people lack heart, but because leaders and institutions have failed. Rather than fretting about support at home, let them show themselves dedicated to waging and winning a strange kind of war and describing it as it is, candidly and in detail. Then the American people will give them all the support they need. The scholar in me is not surprised when our leaders blunder, although the pundit in me is dismayed when they do. What the father in me expects from our leaders is, simply, the truth—an end to happy talk and denials of error, and a seriousness equal to that of the men and women our country sends into the fight.[4]

INSTITUTIONALIZING CYNICISM

In the spring of 2005 the Army tried to do everything it could to avoid recasting the argument as to why people should volunteer. They raised recruiting bonuses to $40,000, offered to pay mortgages for the period of enlistment, dangled promises of a fast track to citizenship, raised the enlistment age to forty-two—just about anything short of winning a date with the general's daughter. The adjustments seemed to be working to the extent that by the end of 2005 fiscal year Army recruitment numbers were better than at the start of the year, even while the war in Iraq continued to lose public support. These efforts had all the appearance of hastily conceived and somewhat panicky Band-Aid "solutions."

JUST ANOTHER CORPORATION?

The old urgent, in-your-face World War II poster, "*UNCLE SAM NEEDS YOU!*" has been changed by today's military to read, "Uncle Sam wants to make you a job offer you might consider. Got a better offer? Okay, sorry to have bothered you." Doesn't have much of a ring to it, does it?

It seems to us that it is as demeaning and shortsighted to pitch the military as a sort of bonus program as it would be if the IRS began to offer mileage points to people who volunteered to pay their taxes. The idea of reducing patriotic duty to a matter of personal choice, job options, and perks on the one hand, while tacitly writing

---

4. Eliot Cohen, "A Hawk Questions Himself As His Son Goes to War," *Washington Post*, July 10, 2005, p. B1.

off Americans who can afford to ignore the bribes on the other, seems to us to spell trouble. But that is more or less what the military's recruiting policy is these days.

Since the recruiting methods are weighted in favor of the job-offer pitch, the military knows it can't compete with "job offers" made to prospective Ivy League graduates (averaging $50,000 starting salaries[5]), so why bother? Besides which, it is too expensive to pay for those Ivy League tuitions; better to take kids from the state schools, where the prices are cheaper. To us this seems to be a capitulation to cynicism.

How we got to this place reflects very badly on our top schools' commitment to our country (as we've discussed, many kicked the ROTC off campus), the military's commitment to fairness (they have given up on the upper classes while concentrating on the "productive" parts of the country, the heartland and small towns), and our government's commitment to the long-term well-being of our armed forces.

In the long term, we as a country need to ask certain questions before we settle for the status quo. What do we lose under the status quo? We diminish the strength of our country's decision making. We lose because of the underdevelopment of character in the upper classes. And we diminish the long-term health of the military. And the military also loses future support.

There are fewer civilian leaders with knowledgeable, hands-on military experience. In other words, the military's future civilian bosses are going to be more ignorant than ever. If present statistical trends continue, we are fast approaching the day when no one in Congress and no president will have served or have any children serving.

If military leaders think this will be good for them and the men

---

5. *Princeton Alumni Weekly,* September 21, 2005, p. 2.

and women they lead, we beg to differ. We predict that the military will be overused and underled and that support will run out fast for any project that becomes a political liability. We predict that if the military leadership thinks that the men and women of the armed services were left twisting in the wind in the last years of the Vietnam War, as the saying goes, they ain't seen nothin' yet! There is a day of reckoning approaching when the military is going to be asked to do the impossible by very misinformed civilian leaders who will not be around to pick up the pieces.

We hope we are wrong. But whatever comes to pass, present trends are already taking a toll. We are losing certain important spiritual intangibles. We are losing fairness and national resolve born of shared sacrifice. We are losing the feeling of national unity and a sustained support for military action that comes only when all our classes serve. Does the military really want to be a force that can only be effective in a hurry-up mode? Will America's enemies take us seriously when each engagement's "success" is tied to a short attention span and the next election cycle? Will a cycle of overextending ourselves, then cutting and running become the permanent "strategy" of the future?

A NEW PERSONAL CONNECTION

The real and symbolic issue of the unarmored Humvees that our troops patrolled the streets of Baghdad in—and were needlessly killed and maimed in—makes the point. It may be almost a cliché to say it, but it seems to us that it is also true to note that if the daughters of, say, President Bush and Bill Clinton had been patrolling the streets of Baghdad with, say, the son of the CEO of the *New York Times,* they likely would have been provided with German- or South African–made armored cars designed for patrolling insurgent-controlled hostile territory—rather than sent out in our woefully underarmored carriers. And it is possible that the civilian leaders who did not listen to the warnings that the Iraq war would turn into a protracted conflict with an insurgency might instead have put together a plan B, just in case their hoped-for outcome of happy Iraqis taking over the running of their country didn't pan out.

One tends to take a worst-case scenario rather seriously if your son or daughter will be on the receiving end. Frank recalls how he sat in John's barracks room and watched John pack up his equipment for his first deployment, and how Frank literally prayed over each piece of protective gear as it was packed, holding a flack jacket in his hands, then atropine injections (the antidote to chemical attack), and then John's Kevlar helmet. The desire to see this equipment work properly was not theoretical. We can't help but feel that our troops would be better served if the last several presidents and many political, business, academic, and media leaders shared Frank's experience.

Our country is better served by a military that is *part of* the democratic experiment in law and spirit, rather than standing apart from it. And here is one more intangible worth considering: If we are in wars with widespread, steady support from members of all classes of society, this sends a strong message to our enemies. That message is: We are all in this together; we will not give up. We are putting our whole nation on the line.

WORST-CASE SCENARIOS

But what if we do not act to change the growing gap? What if we take the themes that we've developed in this book and stretch them to their logical extreme, like the 1940s science fiction writers used to do? We don't pretend to think that we are, in fact, at risk of any of these things happening anytime soon. But these imaginary scenarios may help to clarify what is at stake.

1. *The New American Militarism Meets the Superpower Myth: Superpower ambitions untempered by a feedback loop on military realities lead to imperial overstretch and Great Power decline.*

A letter home from an Army first lieutenant:

September 1, 2036

Hey Parents!

Still kicking butt in the armpit of the world! Sorry, Mom! Things are pretty bad out here—can't lie to you! Thank God for my computer—least I can still get your e-mails—and thank God for 3rd generation Kevlar! The sonsofbitches shut down the friggin military postal service this week to redeploy the postal troops, so don't send me any more baby wipes or hand cleanser. Guess I just have t-learn t-live with my stink! No shower! What with the way things are at home—so we hear— you probably need things as much as I do! OK—Jimmy asked me to answer some questions for his school report. (You still got schools? Ha, Ha!) Yeah, like they tell me anything! It is just so friggin hot! Six dust storms at Camp Zebra in five days! Global warming? The local Hajjis say it's the worst ever, but what do they know. Anyways—the good news and the bad news is we're out—pulling out of Central-friggin-Asia—you've probably seen it on the blogs. You still got blogs, right? I guess the "mission" here's "humanitarian/stabilization"—and we need troop reinforcements for Taiwan, since that shit's gonna blow, to which I say, eat my sushi! Oh yeah, wrong, I know that's the other ones . . . Yeah right—the friggin missile was just "off course"! I got a solution! Let Wal-Mart buy China! Anyways—good news, 'cause—don't think we were doing very well here. Bad news 'cause it'll get worse.

Okay—Jimmy's question—the U.S. has troops all over the world, at least they call them "troops," but you know what

I think of the Air Force—the sun never sets on the U.S. soldier, bla, bla, bla. Around the beginning of the "War on Terror," and what the hell was THAT? Like war on what? War on badness? Like we can't name our friggin enemy?—Anyways, that was then and we had to make the world like us, how global, how inter-friggin-connected we are. I digress. A fly can't burp in China without it spinning up the price of gas in Cincinnati. Sorry Mom—oops!

Okay it's 00:21—I'm back—so this War on Terror never ended and we start the War Against Instability. Lots of a-holes want "stability"—I got your stability right here buddy!—so there's a lot of "international approval" for us busting a gut out here! Right! The U-friggin-N will show up any day, right! Just us and some Nigerians out here—good guys, but their equipment sucks, and THIS is our "coalition?!" Guess you can tell how I feel about it! I hear from my buddies—things aren't any better—Jim's two-thirds of the way finishing up his twenty-six-month deployment to Operation Iraqi Freedom IX—wasn't it supposed to be 3-coups and your out? but, hey, maybe we'll get "democracy," yeah them Shiites really know 'bout that, right?!—says the Green Zone's got electricity 'bout half the friggin day and the Mullahs who took over the south are stepping up the public stonings. You couldn't pay me to be a woman there! Bo an' J.J. are both in Africa. That mission's "expanded"—tryin to end "instability" there too has been sweet! Like playing whack-a-mole! Soon as we clear out a war-friggin-lord an set up a town council somewhere, we move on and the old guys just move on back. J.J.'ll be redeploying to Asia with me. Bo says he thinks they're really ending the famine in Eritrea, but you wonder why we bother—How long till it starts over again? Remember Jen? She's the only one of our group that's stateside—she's at the

Pentagon—sees the money! I remember Dad saying when he was in, the military spent about 4 percent of the country's money! She said it's at like 30–40 percent now, but what do I see for it?! Where is all that shit going? None of our trash works! Let me know if you need me to wire you more money.

Love ya! Later!

2. *An Island Nation in a Sea of Chaos: the undermined military and ambivalent elites . . .*

A letter to my grandchildren:

You are on the brink of graduating high school and college, most of you, and inheriting this world. There's something that's been on my mind that I'd like to share with you. I think my generation made a dreadful mistake.

Around the time you were born, Americans decided to leave the rest of the world alone and asked them to leave us alone. In 2016 a third party, the Libertarian Homefront was the surprise winner in an election that saw both Democrat and Republican parties discredited because of their escalating partisan rancor and corruption scandals that had brought Congress virtually to a halt. The L.H. promised not only less government but less politics, and less policy making, for that matter. Their big idea was that we could have everything each of us wanted, with little interference from politicians. As for peace and security, it was ours if we would give up our overseas military activities. The L.H. pointed out that with recruitment falling, the American people were already voting with their feet, so packing up was the right thing to do.

The L.H. was for personal choice on all issues, all the time. Since everyone got to do what they wanted, everyone seemed content. Religious schools got funding, the right-to-die crowd got death with dignity, anyone could marry anything they chose. If you didn't like how fast everyone was driving after the speed limits were abolished, all you had to do was buy the armor-plated second-generation hybrid Hummer. The L.H. revolutionized our tax forms. From then on, we all got to pick how many shares of our income tax, if any, we would like allocated for various purposes. Those with the most money didn't really want to give much. People never did seem to mark the military share box, and the funds just dried up.

The military was reorganized for explicitly homeland defense and stopped recruiting Americans. Finally, we turned the defense forces into the place where would-be Americans can compete for a chance at citizenship. Most recruiting is now done on the Mexican border and at our embassies all over the world.

We brought our troops home: South Korea wants protection from North Korea—let them figure that out! Taiwan quickly saw the writing and negotiated a "merger" with the mainland. (Rumors are that more than one hundred thousand were executed.) We left Africa, the Caribbean, and Central Asia, and of course had gotten out of Islamic Europe. We closed down the combatant commands of the Pacific region, the Central region, Europe, the Americas, calling them presumptuous on our part. Europe quickly issued conscription for the E.U. countries, and posted the European army along their borders—too late—where they skirmished with crowds of refugees trying to get in from Africa and the Middle East. That happened after the Turks threatened Austria, Germany, and France over an escalating dispute about how the French treated their huge Islamic population (more than 50 percent of their country by 2029). By that point, the Europeans really had no military forces at all, so of course the Turks won concessions in days. As for Israel, well, in ten thousand years the radiation levels should be low enough so archaeologists can dig around in the dust and see if anything is left of the so-called three great religions' holy places! We still don't know who bombed them.

We also increased the INS, and our homeland security focuses on keeping as many illegal immigrants as possible out. We built walls on our borders to help stem the flow, after too many of the border guards were succumbing to bribes from increasingly desperate immigrants.

You may not know that we used to engage throughout the world. We had a strategy to encourage behavior we want in exchange for favorable treatment. It will be hard for you to imagine, but there was a time when we really were very powerful, and both feared and respected. Federal agencies and departments used to provide diplomacy, aid, commercial help, and stability to other countries. California, Alaska, and Oregon were still part of our country. Canada was one country, and there were even exports and imports from places as far off as Saudi Arabia, the old Arabia, that is, before the new caliphate.

As those old cabinet agencies withered, so to did expertise about where and how aid could help America's interests. Without any order, regional powers struggled to assert control, and more and more countries failed. China asserted itself in Asia, saying it had no choice. They amassed nuclear weapons on the Indian-Pakistan border for self-defense, as those countries engaged in a nuclear arms race—India and Pakistan both further increased the size of their militaries in response, and kept large standing armies on their borders. This left the world with fewer consumers and fewer workers, because failed countries can't produce educated workers—they can't produce functioning school systems. Prices skyrocketed in America, as fewer and fewer goods made it into stores.

And so it went. Before you were born, Americans could travel all over the world. Even middle-class people would holiday in Mexico, in Europe, just about anywhere. People had an enormous amount of spending power—closets and closets full of inexpensive clothes, so much so that charities would accept only used clothes in good condition. I know you've heard about this golden age; I wonder if you can even imagine it.

3. *The Military Coup of 2026: Military exceptionalism reaches its logical extreme. (With thanks to Brigadier General Charles Dunlap, Jr., author of the article, "Origins of the American Military Coup of 2001," which inspired this scenario.)*[6]

Dear Jason,

It's been twenty years since you did a foreign officer's exchange program in my unit, and we all teased you so much for your bloody limey accent. Royal Marine, indeed! I'm sure you Brits are wondering how something like this could happen to us, the oldest democracy and all. Anyway, I think the seeds of our own democracy imploding were there long before you and I met.

"In any case," as you might say, the government, the president, Congress, were all viewed with distrust—government was seen as failed. The rich just kept getting richer, and the middle was just trying to get by, not so much silent as just very preoccupied. And both major parties kept pandering to their

---

6. Charles J. Dunlap, Jr., "The Origins of the American Military Coup of 2012," *Parameters* (Winter 1992–93), pp. 2–20.

ideological extremes. People just got sick of the inertia, the stalemate. I was looking at some old notes and saw this comment from the *Atlantic Monthly* of 1991:

> I am beginning to think that the only way the national government can do anything worthwhile is to invent a security threat and turn the job over to the military. . . . According to our economic and political theories, most agencies of the government have no special standing to speak about the general national welfare. Each represents a certain constituency; the interest groups fight it out. The military, strangely, is the one government institution that has been assigned legitimacy to act on its notion of the collective good. "National defense" can make us do things—train engineers, build highways—that long-term good of the nation or common sense cannot. (James Fallows 8/91)

And that was before 9/11! The only major institution that continued to have high marks, from the Gulf War of 1991 on, was the military. The only place this approval level faltered was with the leadership class, of all sectors of society. And the leadership class was increasingly distinct from America at large and more and more ideologically polarized and extreme.

The extent of the disparity between the wealthiest and the middle class was reaching the scale that had existed during the Great Depression. Since then, it's only increased—the leadership class apparently unencumbered by any thought other than the idea that accumulating wealth and/or prestige and passing it on to their own children, deserving or not. And then there was the weird convergence between the three biggest American businesses—oil, gambling, and pornography. Combined, the energy companies, casinos and the biggest porn purveyors controlled a whopping 79 percent of the U.S. economy. This megawealthy superclass—the top 2 percent—came to control nearly 97 percent of the wealth. They lived in gated communities, sent their children in armored limousines to private schools, handed them Mercedeses at age sixteen, and raised a generation concerned only with its own comfort. The "necessities" of the upper class were increasingly items (or services, such as plastic and/or sexual-enhancement surgery) that cost more than a Wal-Mart or McDonald's employee would earn in ten years. And as the wealthy spent their money, they came to look different from everyone else too—endless youth, eternally perky breasts, pouty mouths, and lustrous hair. This hyperextended youth—a lifetime of youth (!)—extended the adolescence of the upper-class children well into their middle age. Yet they "led" us, as the price of running for office continued to skyrocket, so that only the superclass could afford to go into politics.

In the meantime, true to Fallows's prediction, the military started having a larger and larger presence in American society. With the rise of homeland security as a focus, Posse Comitatus, the 1878 law that restricted the U.S. military from operating on our home soil, was rescinded. L.A. was rubble, and so the old rules seemed plain out of date. Who would be next? And after energy prices hit a level where almost half of the ordinary American household budget was consumed by heating and gas bills, people just got crazy. And that was *before* the bird flu pandemic!

The police and FBI continued to feud, and so the public increasingly demanded that the military take over security functions at home. The Army Corps of Engineers repaired the infrastructure damage to the L.A. highways and bridges, so you could at least drive through and get up the coast, though of course you didn't linger! After the military was asked to enforce the bird flu quarantine, the public became more used to seeing uniformed military personnel taking charge in their cities.

Increasingly, too, we military folks were a different caste than the rest. Almost all of us officers came from military families, and most of our wives were from military families too. And we seemed to be the most churchgoing sector of society as well. Enlistees were more likely to come from military-Christian backgrounds too. And most had never even lived off base; it was a cradle-to-grave military life, interrupted only by Bible study and, of course, terrific sports programs, since—not counting the superclass—we military were the only Americans left who could carry our own weight, chronic super-obesity having afflicted about 88 percent of the adult and 76 percent of the adolescent population by then.

Today it's even more extreme. Most people come into the military to make it a career—it's called "the profession of arms" today, no more citizen-soldier—and most grew up in the military. You can always tell. They carry Bibles and can walk without any weight-support implants.

So it seemed like a small step when the military took over. The president was incapacitated during a sixth plastic surgery, and no one really had faith in the vice president, a former star of the hit TV body-building–sexual-marathon reality show, *This Is Your Orgasm*. The head of the Joint Chiefs just started running things, and everyone seemed to breathe a sigh of relief. Most of the military seem to think it's a good idea, that, as godly, disciplined, and fit people, we are better suited to running things anyway, at least for a while until the state of emergency is over. There has been no real protest among the populace though, even to the announcement that there will be no elections scheduled.

I not-so-respectfully dissent—I remember what this country was founded for, and I know we can't get there from here . . . And that is why I'm writing to you from jail. The letter is being smuggled out to you by an old Marine DI I once knew in better times, who is a prison guard now. . . .

9. Solutions

Those who claim their liberty but not their duty to the civilization that ensures it live a half-life, indulging their self-interest at the cost of their self-respect. The richest men and women possess nothing of real value if their lives have no greater object than themselves. . . . Make a sacrifice for a cause greater than self-interest, however, and you invest your life with the eminence of that cause.[1]

—Senator John McCain

Frank and Kathy

We have no illusion that we have the wisdom to propose *the* answers to the problem of the growing gap between those who serve and those who do not. In this chapter are the humbly offered suggestions

---

1. John McCain, "Patriotism Means Reaching beyond Our Self-Interest," in *United We Serve,* ed. E.J. Dionne, Jr., Kayla Meltzer Drogosz, and Robert E. Litan (Brookings Inst., 2003) p. 67.

of two members of the military family, two Americans who've been on both sides of the divide.

There is an unspoken assumption that the only way to get those who have "better options" into the military is to force them. Maybe. Frank favors a type of draft, and Kathy does not. However, whatever the country decides in the future, we propose that the country—those who have access to the bully pulpits of elected office, mass media, celebrity, those who hold some influence in their neighborhoods and living rooms—ask the educated, talented, and privileged young people of America to join their (likewise) talented middle- and working-class brothers and sisters in the trials and glory—and above all, in the responsibility—of wearing their nation's colors. Moreover, we propose that we not only ask them but restructure aspects of our public life and our military recruiting to that end.

Since the Vietnam War we have not even tried to make the case to our most privileged young people for why they should consider service. We seem to have just accepted the received "wisdom" that the upper classes will reject military service out of hand.

The country does not need that many of its most privileged young people to join for it to make a difference. If one in a hundred could see himself or herself learning to lead others, being part of a team, and making his or her mission be the greater good—then those few young people by themselves could create a tipping point. They would become part of the tradition embodied by families such as Franklin Roosevelt's wherein honor, leadership, and privilege walked in step with an ethic of military service. The experience of each of those one-in-a-hundred young people would touch dozens of others in their spheres and, multiplied by each of them, could be nothing less than revitalizing for democracy and accountability.

We do not claim that military service is appropriate for everybody or that a broader military would solve all our problems. And, naturally, we believe there are critically valuable nonmilitary ways to serve our country. We will explore these ways in this chapter. Our point is that *everyone* should at least *consider* serving their country in the military, no matter who they are or what their politics are.

SPECIFICS OF REFORM

To increase participation we must either require it of everyone—an unpopular option now—or couch the need for this service in terms that will inspire our young people. It is our view that service for the benefit of others is a good thing. And as we have argued, it is not good for America that a smaller and smaller proportion of our population carries the load of service for the rest of us, and not just in the military. This fact was borne home again when the Red Cross launched a desperate appeal for forty thousand new volunteers after Hurricane Katrina in 2005. The "usual suspects" were exhausted. And this was happening just as exhausted volunteer soldiers, Marines, sailors, Coast Guardsmen, and airmen were cycled back into duty for rescue efforts just days or weeks after returning home from grueling combat tours in Afghanistan or Iraq. There is something very wrong with this picture.

Below are some good ideas from other people who have been carefully considering how to increase participation in the military and in national service.

1. Reform Current Military Recruiting and Personnel Policy

The U.S. military, quite rightly, sees its job as fighting and winning the nation's wars. Neither the brass nor the sergeants who recruit on the ground are tripping over themselves to sign up the children of the elites. One former head of recruiting that had several Ivy League schools in his district told us that he was constantly fighting for resources, but that if the Army had it their way, they would shut his efforts on these exclusive campuses.

John Lehman, former secretary of the navy under President Reagan, commented that he is frequently asked for help by outstanding students who have gotten a cold shoulder from recruiters; some have been put off for years. He reports that Navy recruiters try to deter anyone who won't make a career commitment to the service at the officer level, including Ivy Leaguers, who are perceived as "short-timers." For instance, a candidate who wants to fly for the Navy must agree to ten years of active duty. Few people with ambitions in the civilian world would take on that kind of commitment.

The solution, says Lehman, is "to take the recruiting policy away from the green-eyeshade bureaucrats who want only lifers, and restore common sense. We should actively seek to attract the most talented from all backgrounds with service options that allow them to serve their country and experience the character-building unique to military service without having to commit to six to ten years of active duty. Under present policies, naval and military service is being, in Gibbon's words, 'degraded to a trade.' "[2]

The burden of who serves in the military should not just devolve to the twenty-five-year-old sergeant who has a quota to fill. People are inspired by those they know, or those they can relate to. If we want to recruit among high-achieving young people, we should consider sending young alums of top colleges who are in the service on a speaking tour of like campuses, in civilian clothes, to talk to their peers honestly about their experiences. And when a political leader is talking on a campus, say one of the many senators or former presidents offering a commencement speech at a place like Columbia or Wellesley, they should promote the idea of military service to a generation of Americans who have never been asked.

---

2. John Lehman, "Degraded into a Trade," *Washington Post,* January 26, 2003, p. B7.

The government should consider making public service announcements in which famous Americans speak about the value of their military service to them. Has anybody asked Colin Powell, Gene Hackman, or George H. W. Bush to do something like this? Why not? The purpose would be, not to recruit for a particular service, but to present the benefits of military service to people who seek inspiration from acknowledged role models and acquaint them with the reality that service did not die out with their grandfather's generation.

Right now, there are a limited number of ROTC slots in the country. Nearly half of all slots are in schools in the South, almost all are allocated to state universities. It is far easier to get an ROTC scholarship from certain small Christian southern schools than it is to win one of a few slots allocated to Princeton. That makes sense if all you care about is body yield per dollar, but not if you want to be as competitive as possible, and not if you want to recruit across classes (and regions).

Professor Richard Kohn of the University of North Carolina-Chapel Hill suggests we make ROTC a floating scholarship, unattached to any particular school, as has been the case in the past. Students would compete for it nationally, based on merit, and take it to the educational institution of their choice. Win the scholarship and you can go to Berkeley, Brown, Bowling Green, or wherever, as long as you are within striking distance of an ROTC program.

Lieutenant Colonel (retired) Mike McCarville, former director of Army ROTC at Princeton, suggests that the services could increase their share of top students at no cost to the military simply by allowing students to choose their career field. Right now, the Army will not guarantee a top engineering student a slot in the Army Corps of Engineers, or a student with stellar academic and physical-fitness levels to choose whether he or she goes to military intelligence or to fly a helicopter.

2. Change Federal Student Aid: Introduce a Tax Credit

The current system of federal financial aid grew out of the G.I. Bill, but now, as Charles Moskos has pointed out, it is "a G.I. Bill without the G.I." He proposes reinstating its original intent as a vehicle for rewarding veterans for their service and making federal financial aid contingent on providing some service to your country. Along similar lines, the Progressive Policy Institute, a Washington, D.C.–based think tank associated with the Democratic Leadership Council, has proposed a college tax credit that would provide a $3,000-a-year credit to students for four years of college and two years of graduate school in exchange for two years of service. We think both these ideas make a great deal of sense, except we would suggest much more generous benefits that would put these programs at the top of the list for any family.

3. Scale Up the Army Citizen-Soldier Option

In October 2003, the military recruited its first citizen-soldiers through a law sponsored by Senators John McCain and Evan Bayh (and suggested by Charles Moskos) that enables volunteers to sign up for fifteen months of service on active duty (after basic and advanced training), followed by twenty-four months in the reserves, and then either a period of availability in the nondrilling Individual Ready Reserves or civilian service in AmeriCorps or the Peace Corps. This short-term program already has a much higher percentage of college-educated and college-bound enlistees than traditional programs.

The initial class of citizen-soldiers had only 3,600 participants. We need to scale this program up, and add an officer component. This program could provide needed reinforcements to the currently overdeployed Army and Marine Corps. With an ability to scale up or down quickly because of the reserve component, it would be much less expensive than adding to overall active-duty end strength (that is, it would cost less than adding more soldiers).

4. Create a National Service Lottery

William Galston, a professor, former domestic-policy adviser to President Clinton, and former draftee who served as an enlisted Marine, suggests a system of compulsory, full-time, eighteen-month service for all fit eighteen-year-olds, either after high school gradua-tion or upon their eighteenth birthday. As an alternative to universal service, Galston suggests a lottery in which there are no exemptions (except for those unfit for any service). Galston explains his rationale for this plan as follows:

> A modern democracy combines a high level of legal equality with an equally high level of economic and social stratification. It is far from inevitable, or even natural, that democratic lead-ers drawn disproportionately from the upper ranks of society will understand the experiences or respect the contributions of those from the lower ranks. It takes integrative experiences to bring this about. In a society in which economic class largely determines residence and education and in which the fortunate will not willingly associate with the rest, only nonvoluntary institutions cutting across all class lines can hope to provide such experiences. If some kind of sustained mandatory service doesn't fill this bill, it is hard to see what will.
>
> Creating this program will be neither cheap nor easy. But consider that we have spent decades creating programs that en-hance individual self-improvement, consumption, and choice. If we work as hard to foster an ethic of contribution and

reciprocity, we can create a richer civic culture that summons, in the words of Lincoln, the better angels of our nature.[3]

Galston sees a lottery affecting at least 20 percent of each cohort of physically and mentally eligible eighteen-year-olds, with no exemptions. He argues that if the lottery has widespread involvement and very few receive an exemption, then more people will buy into it. Participants would choose the military or civil option. If young people did not volunteer in sufficient numbers to satisfy the military's needs, the armed forces would select from among the rest of the pool. Conversely, if the military option filled up first, participants would choose among the remaining domestic options. The period of service would last twelve to eighteen months.

5. Universal Service I: Military and National Service

Economist Robert Litan of the Brookings Institution has proposed a system in which all young Americans participate in service for the country. Those who choose military service would serve two years and receive greater benefits, the rest would do one year of national service in a domestic area. Litan argues:

> Universal service could provide some much needed "social glue" to an embattled American society that is growing increasingly diverse—by race, national origin, and religious preference—and where many young Americans from well-to-do families grow up and go to school in hermetically sealed social environments. . . . Universal service would promote civic

---

3. William A. Galston, "The Case for Universal Service," in *The AmeriCorps Experiment,* ed. Will Marshall and Marc Porter Magee (Washington, D.C.: Progressive Policy Institute, 2005) p. 99.

engagement, which, as Harvard social scientist Robert Putnam has persuasively argued in *Bowling Alone,* has been declining.[4]

Also, he says, through the civic component of this service, we could improve the reading skills of tens of millions of Americans, clean up blighted neighborhoods, help provide social, medical, and other services to elderly and low-income people and families. And lastly, this service would firmly establish the notion that rights for ourselves come with responsibilities for others. Litan estimates this program would carry a cost of $70 billion, though he further estimates the benefits would offset much if not all of that.[5]

6. Universal Service II: Manning the Homefront and Policing Abroad

Charles Moskos and Paul Glastis propose a draft, not for combat soldiers, but for noncombat positions and to address the increased needs on the homefront that emerge from the War on Terror.[6]

Moskos and Glastis propose a draft to provide federal armed personnel to guard dams, nuclear power plants, sports complexes, and U.S. embassies abroad; more border-patrol and customs agents to keep terrorists and their weapons from entering the country; more INS agents to track down immigrants who have overstayed their visas; more Coast Guard personnel to inspect ships; more air marshals to ride on passenger jets; and more FBI agents to uncover terrorist cells operating within and outside our borders.

Overseas, the new draftees could take on duties such as

---

4. Robert E. Litan, "The Case for Universal Service," in *United We Serve,* p. 101.

5. For instance, a Government Accounting Office cost-benefit analysis of AmeriCorps cited a study showing quantifiable monetary benefits of $1.68 to $2.58 for ever dollar invested in three AmeriCorps programs.

6. Charles Moskos and Paul Glastis, "Now Do You Believe We Need a Draft?" *Washington Monthly,* November 2001, pp. 9–10.

peacekeeping. Some of these jobs—patrolling neighborhoods, arresting troublemakers, being first responders in natural disasters, intervening in disputes with a minimum of force—don't require as many special skills as do some complex front-line combat jobs. The authors estimate recruits would need two months of basic training and four months of special police training, before they would be shipped off for an average tour of duty of about six months.

This would free up professional soldiers (and police, FBI agents, and others) to fight the war on terrorism, let alone to respond to whatever inevitable surprises lurk in our future as the world's sole great power, without requiring that the U.S. abandon other vital commitments. It would relieve the drain on the reserves, or could provide personnel to replace those reservists who leave positions back home as firefighters and emergency medical technicians.

Moskos and Glastis point to the additional benefit to the budget—this could ameliorate the need to increase military end strength. Short-term, unmarried volunteers would not have the intense needs that the professional military has for family housing, family health care, retirement benefits, and so forth. As they describe the program:

> One can imagine a similar three-tiered system of youth service in America, with 18-month terms of duty for all citizens age 18 to 25. In this new-style draft, conscripts would have what all Americans now demand: choice. They could choose to serve in the military, in homeland security, or in a civilian national service program like AmeriCorps (there's no reason women couldn't be drafted for the latter two categories). In return, draftees would get GI-bill-style college scholarships, with higher awards for those who accept more dangerous duty.
>
> The best way would be to require all young people to serve. . . . If everyone were required to serve, no one would feel like a sucker.

No doubt there are other, excellent, ideas, which we did not capture here. We hope to learn about them—the more ideas, the better.

OUR DEBATE

We are calling here for a national discussion on our all-volunteer professional versus citizen armed forces. We'll kick off the debate ourselves, with the issue of whether or not to have a draft.

Kathy

After twenty years in politics, I can't help but be pragmatic. In the United States, we are very far from having the political will to create a compulsory program for any kind of national service—military or otherwise. Also, any kind of compulsory program would be very, very expensive, even one that involved a lottery instead of universal service, in part because we'd need to create a whole new government bureaucracy to do it. That money would have to come from some where, and we have a huge budget deficit these days.

So, I don't want to draft our privileged young people. Actually, I'd like to do something even more radical. I'd like to *ask* them to serve.

We who want a more class-representative military can do more to argue for our idea, and we can try to get the government to argue for it too. Because I don't think military service is bitter medicine—I stand by the idea that a period of service, short or long, can be a great experience—so I'd like to try to convince folks, not force them. I believe there are enough privileged young people who will step up to the plate, if asked. As military sociologist Michael Meese commented to me one day, young people today are not anti-military, they are a-military—they don't know anything about the military, or what service entails. So, let's remove barriers, reach out, and demonstrate that military service is a national priority. We should include a national service option to provide the character benefits to those whom military service does not suit. And yes, we should provide a system of educational awards for that service. Then let's see what happens. If that fails, *then* let's come back to a draft.

The word "draft" scares people. Witness the frenzied response (and not only among the upper classes) when the Internet rumor spread before the 2004 elections that George W. Bush had a secret plan to institute the draft. *My* fear is that the public's fear of the draft will completely distract from and overwhelm the important point we are trying to make. That point is that young adults with excellent prospects have many reasons to consider service to their country in the military, and the country should encourage and embrace that service—for the good of the nation as a whole.

Frank

I think we need a draft by lottery that will include all American young people. All would serve in either the military or a civilian capacity. There would be no exemptions except for ill health or severe disability. Even those convicted of nonviolent crimes would be called to serve in some way. The lottery aspect would determine who got called to the military and who got called to the civilian component. A provision for conscientious objectors would be made by allowing them to serve in the civilian component.

It will take strong medicine to break the self-reinforcing cycle of selfishness presently endemic to this culture. It is ironic that Kathy—the Democrat—is calling for volunteer participation, while the Republican in this duo is proposing a big government solution to the problem of defense and service. But I think the last thing we need is more genuflecting to self-expression. I draw on my own past character failures in this regard for proof.

Before my son volunteered, nobody could have convinced me that it would be a good idea for him to serve in the military, not even

Kathy, let alone some politician. I've never helped build a house for Habitat for Humanity. But I *have* faithfully paid my taxes because I don't want to go to jail. Sometimes an individual or country needs what the Marines call "motivation!"

Kathy and I agree that in some areas society has the right to compel people to do things. The only issue is what the circle of compulsion should include.

If duty is explained and if sacrifice is fairly shared, perhaps America won't balk, or at least not most of America, even if there are very noisy protests at first. I also hope a draft will help keep us out of stupid elective wars by upping the ante on our political leadership. My proposal still leaves room for currently all-volunteer parts of the military such as the Marine Corps, Navy Seals, and the Army Special Forces.

I can't be the only American sick and tired of being pandered to by both parties. Message to our leaders: *Please* ask us to do something more for our country than feel good about ourselves.

Frank and Kathy

Okay, so much for our differences. We both believe that whether voluntary or mandatory, national service should have a civilian non-military component. And we think that this would actually be good for the military. *It might free the military to stick to its core mission.*

OUR CONCLUSIONS

Laying aside a debate over a draft, we propose the creation of a "National Service Gateway" by combining the mandatory Selective Service System, military recruiting for all four services (each of which would recruit for regular recruits and for "citizen soldier" recruits), and recruiting for AmeriCorps, the Peace Corps, and even some nongovernmental entities like the Red Cross. All young Americans (male and female) would register for this gateway as young men currently register for Selective Service on their eighteenth birthday as required by the Solomon Amendment. The gateway would be a one-stop shopping outlet for information about and recruiting for both the military and the civilian services.[7] Young people would receive information in the mail about these services, the same way they do for colleges.

Benefits should include college aid to replace current federal student aid (a G.I. bill *with* the G.I.). Those who enter the system after college could receive loan forgiveness. There could possibly be other good results, including a social security benefit for those who serve and/or health-care access. The benefits could be different for military versus civil service, with military service always giving the participant the maximum privileges.

Service, we agree, should be at least twelve to eighteen months or even as much as twenty-four to forty-eight months. It should entail a serious commitment to making our country a better and safer place. And whether it is voluntary or not, a person would be able to choose broadly what kind of job they were signing up for—but the focus would not be on the value of the experience for the individual, rather it would be on the value of the individual's contribution to society. Service would be tough. There would be no easy or completely safe choices. Everyone would risk something real. It would be designed to meet real needs. Satisfaction would be found in serving others, in the camaraderie that military people describe, and finally in that intangible but real sense of having a stake in one's country. Pay would be low. Hours would be long. Discipline infractions would be punished, even for those in the civilian component. There would be a tough boot camp part of training for the civilian options.

---

7. The Progressive Policy Institute has made a very similar suggestion for replacing the Selective Service System with a National Service System that recruits for the "citizen-soldier" program, AmeriCorps, and Peace Corps.

And at the end of service—civilian or military—each person would receive either an honorable or dishonorable discharge that would affect their prospects.

We both agree that the common shared experience of having a great deal expected of you, working to meet a physical and mental challenge, and the readjustment of one's mind from a me-centered universe to broad community awareness and the ideal of shared responsibility and teamwork for a cause greater than oneself would benefit future generations of Americans immeasurably. It would also create a better class of leaders.

We believe that those who choose military service—within the framework of a draft or as an altogether voluntary choice—should be rewarded in a special way for the additional risk and time commitment necessary. For instance, there could be a long term tax incentive that would demonstrate that the nation is truly grateful. And perhaps those who have served for four years or more in the military should receive discounted or free college education in *both* private and public institutions that they qualify for academically.

We have written at length about what the military does. Here are some ideas—in no particular order—about where civilian service, voluntary or as the result of a draft, could make a big difference to our country as well.

* Auxiliary peacekeeping and nation-building forces to do the non-lethal and nonmilitary jobs and democracy promoting tasks internationally.
* Rescue work in natural disasters, and civil defense preparedness for all disasters, natural or otherwise.
* Teaching assistants for teachers throughout America to reduce the number of students per adult in all classrooms by half.
* Uniformed, unarmed auxiliary police patrols, of the kind presently employed in some New York City neighborhoods, to triple

or quadruple the number of uniformed officers on every street in America.

* Augment public works projects such as environmental cleanup, road repair, construction and maintenance of parks, and recreational areas.

* Civilian service workers could check shipping containers or the bags and parcels of more subway riders.

* Civilian forces could boost auxiliary border patrols.

* Preschool child care could be something that tens of thousands of Americans could be involved in with almost no physical ability requirement; this might go a long way to solving the child care dilemma faced by many working parents.

* Volunteers with special skills could supplement primary school and high school curriculums in the arts, music, drama, nature conservancy, and many other enriching programs.

* A vast array of after school and antigang programs could get a boost.

These are just some of the many forms of service that could make a difference to the quality of American life for generations to come. And yes, these would be government projects. The right would have to adjust its antigovernment reactions to such programs, and the left would have to get used to the idea of being boosters of military service. But a rediscovery of a sense of fairness, community, and shared sacrifice might just convince enough Americans of all political stripes to forge a new social contract.

Regardless of whether we adopt a draft or ask people to volunteer, it should become socially desirable to first pay your dues before moving from high school into college or from college to career. It should also become as unthinkable to skip service, as say, telling racist jokes at a party. Social pressure is a very convincing force, for good or ill. Military and/or civilian service should just be one of those things that people take for granted, something like showing up for jury duty.

A LAST WORD . . .

Frank has a friend who regularly tells him that he disagrees with all our current military involvements, but "if the Chinese invade, then I would be the first to volunteer!" What Frank's friend never seems to consider is that if the nation is invaded, it would be a little late to raise an army, or that we might not face the threat at all if the military is kept strong and demonstrates its lethal capability convincingly when the stakes are not quite so high.

When President Clinton was in office, even those soldiers who disliked the president carried out his orders. And the same was and has been true for Presidents Bush—father and son. And it must continue that way for the sake of democracy in the future. The legitimacy of the military does not rest on whether America is led by a "deserving" commander in chief. Our country cannot pursue its policies by only soliciting politically like-minded volunteers: "Who wants to do peacekeeping in Africa? Who's up for hunting Islamist terrorists cave by cave in the Middle East? Anyone want security and stabilization in East Asia?

The people who are most critical of our military on moral grounds could perhaps best effect change by calling on the children of the self-proclaimed "enlightened" to serve, rather than fighting to keep them out. For instance, one who is convinced that prisoner abuse is "systemic" in the military should seek to bring well-educated young people with a keen sense of individual rights to volunteer to be military prison guards, their officers, and the JAG attorneys who prosecute wrongdoers. One would think that the ACLU would be doing everything it could to get military recruiters into places like

Harvard Law School. And those who charge that the military has too many evangelicals should consider that perhaps it is because evangelicals promote the idea of military service where others do not. Here is one solution to any one religious or political group's having undue influence in the military: Make sure those that raise their kids to be Democrats, atheists, agnostics, Jews, Buddhists, Hindus, Muslims, mainline Protestants, liberal Roman Catholics, or progressive Greek Orthodox urge their sons or daughters to join!

Do you want there to be more brass that speak truth to power and stand up to the president about the grave consequences of potential foreign entanglements? Volunteer yourself and make a career of military service, and become that general who leads from the front and helps shape national policy for a generation. And if you aim for the cabinet level, consider a tour of duty first. You may find you have more to contribute because of your prior service, something you may have learned about the world and the people around you.

The more critical someone is of the military or our actions using our military, the more they are bound—if they want to be taken seriously—to encourage broad military participation. It is after all, *our* military, not someone else's. And for those who wave the flag and support the troops but also consider their own family exempt from service because of the wealth of options available to them, we suggest they take the magnetic yellow ribbon off their SUV and rethink their position.

We began this book concerned with how losing the leadership class's involvement on the front lines of our military policy hurts our country—hurts our policy making and undermines its legitimacy. Along the way we have come to believe that when it comes to citizenship, the only real way for a citizen to have ownership in his or her country is through sweat equity.

Our military men and women are doing work that should be shared by many more people. Maybe someday a soldier can come home to a mother, father, lover, husband, wife, or newborn child a precious month earlier from a far-distant deployment because somebody else did their share. Maybe someday some soldier will survive a battle because someone very talented, educated and imaginative turned out to be a great officer instead of rushing right into that lavishly remunerated law office or Wall Street job. Maybe those soldiers will not have to face combat at all because our unity has made us more formidable.

It has been a wonderful experience for us to lay aside differences of opinion and fight—if that is the right word for two people who have done no more than type!—for something we believe in next to a person whom we might be fighting *with* if it weren't for an overriding cause. And to us that "cause" is the long-term health of our country's defenses and the men and women who guard us all.

We have both cried with joy at the sight of a beloved figure coming home. And those men—one a young son and one a middle-aged husband—wore the same uniform. We have also wept for the friends who will never again see the beloved face of someone they sent off with so many heartfelt prayers. What on earth could we find to argue about that would override that? And to us, this life lesson has pointed us to a larger truth: we really *are* all in this together.

Meanwhile there are ever-faithful young American men and women who are guarding us while we Americans argue about what it means to *be* Americans. That is how it should be. May the argument continue! We know the members of our steadfast military who are defending the precious right to argue among ourselves are worthy of a great country. We know they are worthy of the greatest respect. We hope we become more worthy of those men and women.

Acknowledgments

We thank Jennifer Lyons, our agent, who was immediately enthusiastic about this project. Thank you to Smithsonian publisher Don Fehr and to our editor Elisabeth Dyssegaard, who has been a joy and inspiration to work with.

We would also especially like to thank General (ret.) Tommy Franks and his wife, Cathy Franks, for their encouragement and support. And many thanks to Cathy Franks for very carefully going through an early draft of the book line by line and providing many specific suggestions.

A number of military sociologists, historians, and political scientists were very generous with their time in listening to our argument, giving advice, and correcting our manuscript in its various forms. We would like to specifically thank professors Peter Feaver and Richard Kohn, whose seminal survey work is cited extensively in this book and who spoke with us on many occasions. Professor Charles Moskos is the dean of military sociologists; he provided us with references, read our manuscript, and gave us guidance. Our work significantly benefited from the advice of professors Andrew

Bacevich and Jim Burk and Colonel Michael Meese. Professor Donald Zillman not only provided excellent scholarly advice, he gave his time very generously in editing the manuscript. Thanks also to professor Eliot Cohen and Michael O'Hanlon of the Brookings Institution for their interest and good thoughts on this project. Thanks also to Dee Dee Myers for her time and support.

Kathy would not have gotten to the point of writing this book without the advice and generosity of Bruce Kluger, who helped her get started writing. Thanks also to *USA Today* commentary editor John Siniff who went above and beyond in encouraging these ideas.

Many people helped us develop our ideas. Kathy's husband, Lieutenant Colonel Greg Douquet, has been especially helpful. John Schaeffer, Frank's son, who served in the Marines, not only inspired Frank to write this book but also contributed several long quotes. Thanks also to Lieutenant General (ret.) Earl Hailston, who has been patient and available as a sounding board. Kathy's former boss and good friend John Goodman and his wife, Sherri Goodman, helped Kathy navigate and understand the Pentagon when she worked there and provided her with much good advice on the civilian side of military affairs. Thank you to Holly Page of the Democratic Leadership Council and Progressive Policy Institute—she has been an excellent source.

We owe a big thank you to the wives and the Marines of HMM 264 and of MAG-26 and MAG-29, many of whom shared their wisdom and supported this effort. And thank you to Kathy's plucky "mother's helpers," Christine Greeno and Erica Sucameli—this book would not have been possible without them. Thanks for the patience of Kathy's children, Sophie and Charley, and the forbearance of Greg, who left for war with a wife who was a sometimes-lawyer, and returned to find himself married to a writer.

During one of Frank's extended stays on Parris Island researching material for this book, many Marines and recruits were most helpful. Among them (listed in the order Frank met them) were Major Ken White, Major Keith Burkepile, First Sergeant Lawrence Finneran, Staff Sergeant Elliot, Sergeant Guerrero, Staff Sergeant Maynor, Staff Sergeant Itnalia, Staff Sergeant Coons, Sergeant Silva, Staff Sergeant Potter, recruits Torres and Petersen, Staff Sergeant Timothy Soignet, recruit Jackie Allberty, Colonel Kevin Kelley, Sergeant Major John Wylie, Staff Sergeant Sherri Battle, Sergeant Tammy Shelton, and Sergeant Ortiz. We are sorry that we don't know all these Marines' current rank or even most of their first names. Frank was jotting names as best he could while trying to keep up with hard-charging Marines and recruits!

We owe a special debt of thanks to Staff Sergeant, Senior Drill Instructor George Henderson (ret.). He was Frank's son's SDI on Parris Island. George Henderson took the time to let Frank interview him.

We are also grateful to Mike Strobl, Brenda Copeland, Max Boucher, John Raughter, Will Marshall, Susan Bell, Maureen McNeill, Gary Bauer, and last, but certainly not least, Genie Schaeffer.

Thank you all so much!